Enneagram Test

The Complete Guide to Understanding the 9 Types of Personality with the Sacred Enneagram. Insight approach to understanding and explaining human behavior. Discover Who You Are and Who You Can Be

BY

Travis Henderson

Table of Contents

CHAPTER ONE...3

WHAT IS ENNEAGRAM?...................................6

Where does the enneagram come from?...........50

Wing Types...58

CHAPTER TWO...70

THE NINE PERSONALITY TYPES............................70

The enneagram test.................................151

CHAPTER THREE...161

HOW CAN YOU FIGURE OUT WHAT TYPE OF PERSONALITY YOU ARE?..............................161

CHAPTER FOUR..173

Help with identifying your enneagram.............173

type and identifying your personality.................194

CHAPTER FIVE...200

Type On Your Own The Results And After Getting The Results...200

CONCLUSION...204

The information provided herein is stated to be truthful and consistent, in that any liability, in terms of inattention or otherwise, by any usage or abuse of any policies, processes, or directions contained within is the solitary and utter responsibility of the recipient reader. Under no circumstances will any legal responsibility or blame be held against the publisher for any reparation, damages, or monetary loss due to the information herein, either directly or indirectly.

Respective authors own all copyrights not held by the publisher.

The information herein is offered for informational purposes solely and is universal as so. The presentation of the information is without contract or any type of guarantee assurance.
The trademarks that are used are without any consent, and the publication of the trademark is without permission or backing by the trademark owner. All trademarks and brands within this book are for clarifying purposes only and are the owned by the owners themselves, not affiliated with this document

CHAPTER ONE

WHAT IS ENNEAGRAM?

The Enneagram is a system of personality typing that Clarifies routines in the way folks conceptualize the planet and manage their own emotions. The Enneagram model identifies two distinct personality types and maps every one of this type on a nine-pointed diagram that helps to exemplify the way a type relates with another. The name Enneagram arrives from the Greek: Ennea could be that the Greek word for Gramma means something which is written or drawn.

According to the Enneagram, each character has a particular World perspective and discusses the world through their particular filter or lens. This helps make it feasible to spell out why folks act in certain manners. By explaining the way, the simple character reacts and reacts to both supportive and stressful scenarios, the Enneagram shows chances for private development and gives a base for your understanding of the others.

The Enneagram is a system of nine personality forms blending conventional wisdom with contemporary psychology - a stronger tool for understanding ourselves and the people in our own lives - together with three Main programs:

Personal and religious development

Powerful relationships in the home and in the Office

Leadership Enhancement, team building and communication abilities for company

Enneagram Work provides the knowledge and tools:

Increase your own personal and professional efficacy

Boost Your self-awareness and psychological intelligence

Know your own patterns of thinking, feeling and acting

Build effective relationships in your home and in the Office

Encourage your strengths, and identify your blind areas and also handle private reactivity

Construct your internal life

A Concise History

This Nine-pointed diagram (Ennea is Greek for two) has reportedly been used for hundreds of years in literary Christian and Sufi traditions because of hint of individual comprehension and archetypes.

It had been First attracted to people at 1915, in Moscow, by George Gurdjieffa philosopher and educator who used it within his schedule of individual improvement. Subsequently from the late 1960s, Oscar Ichazo, the creator of this Arica School, put nine Kinds of character on the Enneagram. Shortly afterwards, Claudio Naranjo, MD, along with different psychologists from Berkeley united the Enneagram with the most recent improvements of contemporary psychology.

Even though Each personality kind are discovered in psychological literature, so the Enneagram attracts them together in a unified system and also shows their own inter relationships. This mixture of ancient emblem and contemporary psychology is still developed now by psychologists, industry advisers, teachers and spiritual supervisors.

A Non-Denominational System

From its own Ancient origins in Berkeley, today's Enneagram has spread across the globe with greater than just a thousand books sold and Enneagram apps or institutes in many states in Europe and East Asia, in addition to elements of Africa and South America. As the Enneagram itself does not imply a specific ideology, theology or collection of processes, it functions as a quite effective conceptual platform for both secular professionals and spiritual clergy within their own work with customers or congregants.

Unlike Most emotional systems and analytical tools that give attention to the problem side of the public, the Enneagram perhaps not merely speaks about the conditions which individuals face, in addition, it explains the strengths and capabilities of each and every personality style. No personality type isn't any worse or better, along with the highs and lows of individual evolution are available in most type.

While many People today understand that the Enneagram being a deep system of spiritual or personal growth, in modern times in addition, it was adapted for use within the classroom and the company atmosphere. Along with supplying essential "people skills," that the Enneagram encourages self-awareness, fantastic decision-making, and consistent learning that's essential for success in the current workplace.

Disposition and Essence

A secret Idea underlying the Enneagram is people have just two major aspects - character and personality.

Each individual has an original "fundamental self" that cannot be paid down to lots or category. Nevertheless, that the Enneagram describes two different patterns or motifs from which people sort a personality, and also a societal character, to match with the challenges of work and love. Ideally, personality can be definitely an efficacious means to express ourselves from the entire world. But problems arise if personality covers the inner ego, or so our point of perspective gets rigid and stuck.

Three Centers of Intelligence

The Enneagram describes three centres of intellect and understanding: Head, Heart and human body. While every man has three of those centers, all those nine personality types includes a specific strength in a few. Our internal personality arrangement in addition to our manner to be on earth relies in this particular leading, or main centre. Recognizing our principal center can be an essential key for developing our professional and personal potential and beating blind areas.

The Intellectual Center: Employing the brain for speech and logical thinking, ideas and graphics, strategies and approaches. Located Within the face area.

The Emotional Center: Employing the "hub" for favorable and negative emotions, compassion and concern for others, devotion and romance. Located Within the Region of the diaphragm and chest.

The Instinctual Center: employing your human body for movement, sensate comprehension, gut amount knowing, personal security and societal belonging.

Structure

Even the Enneagram's structure might seem complex, though it Is obviously straightforward. This can allow you to comprehend that the Enneagram in the event that you sketch yourself.

Draw a ring and then indicate nine equidistant points its circumference. Designate each point with way of a few from one to eight, with eight at the very top, for symmetry and from tradition. Each point represents just one of those eight basic personality types.

The Enneagram, literally, can be really a sign. It's a nine-pointed emblem that's shown up in lots of religions throughout the past couple of millennia. Nobody knows for certain the ancients developed the analysis or the way they used it before very recently. Enneagram Spectrum sums up the speculations concerning the roots of this enneagram such as this:

"The Origins of the Enneagram are contested. Some writers believe they've discovered variations of this Enneagram emblem while in the sacred geometry of the Pythagoreans that 4000 decades past were interested at the deeper meaning and need for amounts. The lineup of mysterious mathematics was passed through Plato, his disciple Plotinus, and also following Neo-Platonists.

Some Believe this convention found its way to esoteric Judaism through Philo, a Jewish Neo-Platonist philosopher," where it afterward looks like the Tree of Life from the Cabalistic tradition of nine oldness.

Variations Of this emblem appear in Islamic Sufi customs, possibly coming there throughout the philosopher al-Ghazzali. Throughout the fourteenth century that the Naqshbandi Order of Sufism, variously called the "Brotherhood of the Bees" (simply because they accumulated and stored comprehension) and the "Symbolists" (because they educated through symbols) would be claimed to have passed and preserved the Enneagram logo.

Speculation Has it that the Enneagram found its way to esoteric Christianity through Pseudo-Dionysius (who had been influenced by the Neo-Platonists) and throughout the mysterious Ramon Lull (who had been influenced by his own Muslim studies)

On the Frontispiece of a proposal written in the nineteenth century by the Jesuit mathematician and student of arithmology Athanasius Kircher, an Enneagram-like figure looks."

Recently Years, the Enneagram has been"re discovered" from Oscar Ichazo, a Chilean philosopher who taught in the Arica Institute at Chile. Ichazo, in my opinion, was that the first man to really use the legislation of this enneagram into the nine legislation which operate within the individual mind.

The method by which in which the enneagram is comprehended today is it is an instrument to help comprehend and pronounce nine "filters" that somebody can utilize to find the globe. These filters are somewhat fluid, intangibles which might or might not exist in fact, but with these as tools may cause extreme realizations in relationships or even on your own personal growth.

The two things on the circumference will also be attached with every other by the inner traces of the

Enneagram. Be aware that things Three, Six, and form an equilateral triangle. The rest points are attached in the following sequence: One joins using Two, Four with 2 two with two, Eight using Five, Five together with Seven, and Seven with One. These six things form an intermittent hexagram. The significance of those inner lines will probably be discussed briefly.

Your Standard Personality Style

Out of 1 point of perspective, the Enneagram is regarded as a couple of nine different personality types, together with each number over the Enneagram denoting 1 type. It's normal to locate only a little of yourself at each of the types, but certainly one of these should be noticeable to be nearest to your own. Here really is the basic personality style.

Everyone Emerges from youth with just one of those nine types controlling their character, together with inherent character and other non-natural variables function as the principal determinants of this type. That really is 1 area where many everyone the main Enneagram writers agree--we have been born with a dominant type. Afterward, this inherent orientation chiefly determines the manners that we know how to accommodate to your early youth atmosphere. Additionally, it appears to result in certain unconscious orientations supporting our civic amounts, however this is some do not know.

In Almost any circumstance, at the time kids are five years of age, their understanding has grown satisfactorily to get another sense of self. Even though their individuality continues to be quite fluid, as of this age children start to establish themselves in order to discover means of fitting in to the world by themselves.

Several More things can be created about the fundamental type itself.

People don't switch in a personality type to the next.

The descriptions of these personality types are universal and apply equally to men and females, since no type is inherently masculine or feminine.

Perhaps not everything from the description of one's essential type will employ for you all of the time as you change constantly one of the healthy, ordinary, and unhealthy faculties which compose your personality form.

The Enneagram uses amounts to designate all one of these types as amounts are value-neutral -- they also imply the wide assortment of perspectives and behaviors of each type without demonstrating such a thing positive or negative. Unlike labels applied in psychiatry, amounts supply an unbiased, shorthand way of suggesting that a good deal about somebody with no pejorative.

The numerical standing of these types isn't important. A bigger number is better than an inferior number; nevertheless, it really is better to be always a Nine compared to two because nine is really a larger number.

Whatever type is inherently better or worse than every. While all of the personality types have particular resources and obligations, some kinds tend to be regarded as more desired than many others in any particular culture or category. Moreover, for 1 reason or the other, you might well not be happy being a specific type. You will believe that the type will be "disabled" in a manner. Since you know more about all of these types, you are going to understand that as each has particular abilities, each has different limits. If a few kinds are more prestigious in Western society compared to many others, it's due to the qualities which society benefits, but maybe not as a result of some superior significance of the types. The best would be to get to be your very best self, never to mimic the resources of another kind of

The Centers

The Enneagram is a 3 x 3 structure of eight-character Types in three Centers. There are 3 types from the Instinctive Center, three at the Feeling Center, and also three at the Believing Center, as shown below. Each Center is made up of three personality types which have in common the resources and obligations of this Center. By way of instance, personality type Four includes exceptional strengths and obligations involving its own feelings, which explains the reason why it really is from the Center. Likewise, the Eight's obligations and assets demand its own relationship to its instinctual drives, that explains why it really is from the Instinctive Center, etc. for two personality types.

The addition of every enter its Center isn't random. Each kind leads out of the certain romance with a bunch of topics which describe that Center. Quite simply, these dilemmas revolve round a robust, largely unconscious emotional reaction to the increasing loss of touch with the heart of the self. From the Instinctive Center, the emotion will be Anger or even Rage. From the Center, the emotion will be Shame, also at the Thinking Center, It's Stress. Obviously, all nine types comprise each of the feelings, however in each middle, the characters of these kinds are specially influenced by this Center's psychological motif.

Ergo, each form has a Specific manner of coping with all the Dominant Awareness of its Center. We can temporarily see exactly what this means by analyzing every type, Center from Center. From the Instinctive Center, Eights act out their anger and instinctual energies. To put it differently, when Eights feel anger construction inside them, they instantly answer it in some physical method, increasing their voices, even moving forcefully. The others may definitely view that Eights are mad because they provide themselves permission to share their anger.

Nines deny Their anger and instinctual energies as though to say "What anger? I'm not even a Man who has mad." Nines would be the kind most out of contact with their anger and instinctual energies, frequently feeling threatened by these. Obviously, Nines Get mad like everybody, but make an effort to stay out from these feelings that are darker. Focusing on idealizations in their connections and their own world.

Ones Effort To restrain or repress their wrath and energy. They believe they must remain in control of these, especially among these instinctual impulses and mad feelings in constantly. They'd really like to guide these energies in line with the orders of these highly improved inner critic (super ego), the way to obtain these strictures on others and themselves.

From the Center, Twos Effort To restrain their pity by getting different people to enjoy them and also to consider about them as good men and women. Additionally, they desire to convince themselves they truly are good, loving people by emphasizing the positive feelings while the others while repressing their unwanted feelings (such as anger and bitterness at not being valued enough). As-long-as Twos could possibly acquire favorable emotional responses from the others, they believe wanted and also have the ability to get a handle on feelings of pity.

Threes attempt to Deny their pity, and also therefore are arguably the very from touch with inherent feelings of inadequacy. Threes learn how to deal with pity by looking to become the things they believe an invaluable, successful person resembles. So, Threes figure out how to carry out well, so as okay, actually outstanding, and in many cases are driven relentlessly within their quest for succeeding for a means of staving off feelings of pity and fears of failure.

Fours Effort To restrain their pity by simply concentrating on just how special and unique their own specific talents, feelings, and individual traits are. Fours highlight their identity and imagination as a method of handling their black feelings, even although Fours would be the sort most prone to succumb to feelings of inadequacy. Fours additionally manage their pity by nurturing a wealthy, romantic dream life by which they usually do not need to manage anything inside their lifetime appears drab or dull in their mind.

From the Thinking Center, Five S have Fear of the outside world and also about their own capacity to manage this. Ergo, they handle their fear of withdrawing from the globe. Five S grow to be secretive, isolated loners using their heads to permeate in the type of earth. Five S expect that finally, while they know facts in their terms, they'll soon be in a position to rejoin the planet and take part in it, however they never believe that they understand enough to engage with absolute confidence. As an alternative they involve themselves using increasingly complicated internal worlds.

Sixes display The most dread of most three types, chiefly characterized as stress, that induces them to function as probably the very from touch using their sense of inner knowing and optimism. Unlike Fives, Sixes have trouble expecting their own heads, therefore that they are constantly looking out themselves to get something to make them feel sure of these. They may turn into representations, beliefs, relationships, occupations, savings, government, or even some other mixture of those above mentioned. But irrespective of the amount of security arrangements that they make, Sixes still really feel suspicious and stressed. They might even start to doubt that the most men and women and beliefs they have looked into for reassurance. Sixes can also react for their own anxiety and fear from impulsively facing it defying their fear from an attempt to become free from it.

Sevens possess Fear of their inner planet. You will find feelings of melancholy, lack, anxiety, and basic stress that Sevens might love to remain clear as far as feasible. To deal with those feelings, Sevens maintain their heads busy with intriguing options and possibilities -- for as long because they've something exciting to expect, Sevens believe they could divert themselves out of their anxieties. Sevens, generally, don't end only at believing about those options, yet. Just as you possibly can they make an effort to truly do as a lot of the options while possible. So, Sevens could be seen staying on the move, chasing one adventure after another, also keeping themselves amused and participated together with their various thoughts and activities.

The Wing

Nobody is a pure character kind: everybody is a special Mix of her or his elementary type and usually just one of those 2 types adjoining to it upon the circumference of their Enneagram. One of both types next to an essential type is named your wing.

Your fundamental kind dominates your general character, while the wing distinguishes it and adds crucial, sometimes contradictory elements to a complete personality. Your wing would be your "second side" of one's personality, also it has to be taken into account to understand yourself or somebody else. As an instance, if you're a personality type two, then you will probably have a One-wing or an Eight-wing, along with your personality in general can be realized by taking into consideration the faculties of this Seven since they visually blend with the faculties of the main one or the tenth. Inside our instruction experience through time, we also have struck some people who seem to own both limbs, while some have been strongly impacted by their own essential type and reveal bit of wing.

There's debate among the various customs of this Enneagram about if folks have a couple of wings. Simply speaking, everybody else has two limbs in the restricted sense both of those types adjoining to an essential type are operative on your style since each individual owns the abilities of nine different types. But that really is simply not exactly what is ordinarily meant by "with two limbs," and proponents of those so-called two-wing theory genuinely believe both limbs operate just about evenly in everyone else's personality. (by way of instance, they think a Six might have about equal numbers of his / her Eight and something wings)

Tracking of individuals leads us to conclude that although the two-wing Theory pertains for a individual, the majority of people possess a dominant wing. From the great bulk of men and women, as the so-called wing consistently remains operative for a level, the wing is a lot more crucial. (by way of instance, Twos using Three-wings are markedly distinct from Twos using One-wings, also while Twos using Three-wings possess a One-wing, it's not anywhere near as important since the Three-wing.) It's consequently clearer to refer in order to some type's "wing" as compared to its own "dominant wing," since both terms reflect the exact same idea.

1 other observation concerning fires will probably be well worth mentioning. In The path of education that the Enneagram in workshops and also Trainings, a lot of folks while in the latter half their own lives have reported that the evolution of their socalled"2nd wing" And in people who've been chasing spiritual or psychological work, we've found signs that is true. We usually do not understand, yet, if these students ended up only watching each one the positive capacities of their two types unfolding included since they developed --their next wing being clearly one of those additional seven different types --or even if that was a certain evolution of the next wing style. We'll continue to explore this idea in our own work together with your students and coworkers.

It's, of course, essential to spot the fundamental kind Until it's possible to check that wing you've got. Besides signaling your essential type, the Riso-Hudson Enneagram Type Indicator can also signify your own wing. Nevertheless, the ideal method to comprehend the effect of one's wing is always to learn the whole descriptions of one's own type and its own wings in Personality Types. You might even study the descriptions of those 2 types adjoining to an essential type and decide which best pertains to you.

The Quantities of Development

There's an internal arrangement inside every character type. That arrangement could be the continuum of behaviors, attitudes, guards, and motives formed by the two Degrees of Development that comprise the personality type itself. This discovery (and the exercising of all of the faculties which include every type) was originally made by Don Riso in 1977, and has been further improved by Don by Russ Hudson from the 1990s. They truly are the sole Enneagram teachers to add this essential component in their own treatment of their Enneagram. The Degrees are still an essential contribution not just to the Enneagram however also to self-psychology -- and also the personality types of the

Enneagram cannot be adequately explained with them. The Degrees accounts fully for differences between individuals of the identical type in addition to the way that folks change both for worse or better. Ergo, they're also able to help therapists and advisers pinpoint what's clearly going on with customers and indicate methods to the difficulties they have been receiving.

The Amount of Development supply a frame for viewing Just how most the different faculties which include each type squeeze in to a massive whole; nevertheless, they truly are a method of conceptualizing the inherent "skeletal" arrangement of each type. With no Degrees, the types could appear to be a random assortment of unrelated faculties, together with conflicting behaviors and attitudes frequently a portion of this film. However, by understanding the Amounts for every kind, an individual is able to observe exactly how everyone the faculties are interrelated--and also the way that healthy faculties may deteriorate to ordinary faculties and into ones that are unhealthy. As pioneering comprehension philosopher Ken Wilber has noticed, with no Degrees, the Enneagram is paid down to a "flat" pair of nine different categories. By adding the Degrees, but a "vertical" dimension is included not just reflects the sophistication of individual character, but extends much in explaining a variety of, crucial elements in nature.

Further, together with the Degrees, a lively component is introduced That reflects the shifting nature of their personality layouts themselves. You've likely realized that folks change always --they have been somewhat clearer, more lIberated, grounded, and more emotionally offered, while occasionally they have been more nervous, immune, responsive, emotionally volatile and not as free. Knowing the Amounts makes it crystal clear when folks change countries inside their personality, they have been changing within the range of motives, faculties, and defenses which compose their style type.

To know a person correctly, it's necessary to Perceive at which anyone lies over the continuum of Degrees of her or his type at a certain time. To put it differently, an individual has to assess if or not a man or woman is inside their own healthy, moderate, or poor array of functioning. That is important as, as an instance, two different people of the exact same personality type and wing will probably fluctuate considerably if a person is healthy and also the other UN healthy. (In relationships as well as at the world of business, understanding this differentiation is essential.)

The continuum is constituted of two inner Heights of Development--temporarily, you will find 3 Degrees in the nutritious section, three Degrees in the ordinary section, and also three Degrees in the un-healthy section. It could allow one to believe about this continuum of Degrees as a photographer's gray-scale that includes gradations from pure white to black with lots of colors of grey in between. But on the continuum, the lightest traits seem , on very best, so to speak. Once we proceed down the continuum at a spiral pattern we progressively go each amount of Development indicating a different shift from the personality's corrosion to the black of emotional breakdown at the floor. The continuum for all of those personality types is understood from the diagram.

The Continuum of those Quantities of Development

Healthy

· Measure 1: the Amount of Liberation

· Level 2: the Amount of Emotional Capacity

· Measure 3: the Amount of Social Value

Average

· Measure 4: the Amount of Imbalance/ / Social Role

· Measure 5: the Amount of Inter Personal Control

· Measure 6: the Amount of over Compensation

· Amount 7: the Amount of Violation

· Measure 8: the Amount of Obsession and Compulsion

· Level 9: The Amount Of Pathological Destructiveness

At every Level, important psychological changes happen as will be Signaled by the name we've contributed into it. By way of instance, in Level 5, the degree of Interpersonal get a grip on, the man or woman is attempting to govern himself along with other people to receive her or his emotional demands met. This always creates societal conflicts. With this Amount, anyone has fully identified with the self and will not find himself as anything longer than this: the self must hence be defended and inflated to allow the man or woman to feel safe and also to maintain their individuality intact. Whether this activity doesn't meet the individual, and stress grows, they could deteriorate into the following nation, Grade 6, the degree of over-compensation, where their behavior will be much more intrusive and competitive since they carry on to sack their own ego-agenda. Stress is rising, and also the man or woman is disruptive, and dedicated to getting his demands met, irrespective of impact on people across them.

Certainly one of the very profound ways of knowing the Degrees Can be like a step of their capacity to show up . The further people proceed down the Degrees, the more further diagnosed we're using this self and its own negative and restrictive routines. Our personality grows more defensive, responsive, and automatic-- we have less and less real freedom and not as real comprehension. Once we proceed down the Degrees we become trapped in more hurtful, damaging activities that are finally invisibly.

By comparison, the motion toward wellness, upward the Degrees , is with being present and alert inside our heads, hearts, hearts, and bodies. Even as we are present we eventually become fixated from the defensive structures of our personality and also so are somewhat more pliable and more receptive to ourselves and types. We view our character speedily for activity in the place of "falling asleep" into your automated personality routines. There's hence the chance for "not doing" our personality and also of obtaining a few true spaces out of the unwanted effects of getting trapped inside it.

As we are more current, we view that our character Faculties More inexpensively and the Degrees turned into an ongoing guide to self-observation, a map which we may utilize to graph where we have been inside our psycho-spiritual development at any particular time. Even as we proceed "upward" the Degrees we detect we have been far more not as driven by compulsive, subconscious forces and so are ready to act better in every area of our own lives, including our relationships. After we have been diagnosed with all our personality, we discover we respond as crucial to whatever life presents, actualizing the constructive abilities in most two classes, bringing real peace, imagination, strength, happiness, compassion, along with other constructive qualities to anything we're doing.

Instructions of Integration (Growth) and Dis-integration (Stress)

Since We've seen together with all the Quantities of Development the two Personality types of the Enneagram aren't static types: they signify our shift as time passes. What's more, the arrangement of these type s and the structure of these inner lines of this emblem aren't random. The inner traces of this Enneagram join the types in a sequence which refers to what each type is going to do under different problems. There are just two traces linked to every kind, plus so they associate to just two other styles. 1-line joins with a sort that reflects the way the man of this very first type acts whenever they're moving toward growth and health. This can be called the Management of Integration or Growth. One other line would go into some other type that reflects the way the man or woman is very likely to behave if they're under increased stress and anxiety --whenever they believe they aren't in charge of this circumstance. This second point is known as the Management of Anxiety or Disintegration. To put it differently, different scenarios will elicit various sorts of answers in the own personality. You'll respond or accommodate to various directions, according to the traces of this Enneagram in the essential type. We start to see that the flexibility and dynamism of the Enneagram.

The Management of Disintegration or Stress to get Each kind is indicated by the arrangement of amounts 1-4-2-8-5-7-1. This usually means an average to Bad one-under stress will fundamentally act as an average to unhealthy Four; the average to unhealthy Four will probably act out their worry as the average to Match 2; the average to unhealthy 2 will behave out under stress such as an two weeks, an two will behave out under stress just like a twenty five, a Five will probably behave out such as a Seven, and also a Seven will probably behave out just like alone. (A simple way to keep in mind that the arrangement is to appreciate 1-4 or 14 doubles to 28, also that doubles to 5 7 --or nearly so. So, 1-4-2-8-5-7--and also the arrangement contributes into inch and also starts again) Likewise, about the equilateral triangle, the arrangement is 9-6-3-9: a Stressed-out Six will probably behave out just like a Six, a Stressed-out Six will probably behave out just like a Three, and also a Stressed-out Three will probably behave out just like a Nine. (it is possible to remember this arrangement if you imagine about these numerical values decreasing as the ones be much more worried and responsive. For a more explanation and examples, visit Character Types, 47-52, 413-8.) You can see how this works by following the path of the arrows onto the Subsequent Enneagram:

The Management of Disintegration (Stress)

1-4-2-8-5-7-1

9-6-3-9

The Management Of Integration or Development is suggested for each kind by the opposite of those strings for disintegration. Each kind goes toward integration at a way that's the contrary of its bad management. Ergo, the arrangement for its Management of Integration is 1-7-5-8-2-4-1: a incorporating One would go into Seven, an incorporating Seven would go into Five, an incorporating Five belongs into Eight, an incorporating two would go into Two, an incorporating Two would go into Four, as well as also an incorporating Four extends into at least one. On the equilateral triangle, the string will be 9-3-6-9: an incorporating two will proceed into three, an incorporating Three goes to Six, along with an incorporating Six will probably go to . It's possible to observe this operates by following a direction of the arrows onto the subsequent Enneagram.

The Management of Integration (Growth)

1-7-5-8-2-4-1

9-3-6-9

It's not Necessary to possess different Enneagrams for that Management of the Management of Disintegration. Both guidelines can be exhibited using a single Enneagram by removing arrows and linking the appropriate points together with lines that are plain.

The Management of Integration (Growth)

1-7-5-8-2-4-1

9-3-6-9

The Management of Disintegration (Stress)

1-4-2-8-5-7-1

9-6-3-9

No Issue Which character type you're, the types in either Your Management of Integration or Development as well as your Management of Disintegration or Anxiety are most significant impacts. To acquire a comprehensive picture of yourself (or someone else), you must take under account the fundamental kind and wing in addition to both the 2 types from the Instructions of Integration and Disintegration. The facets represented by people four types blend to a complete personality and offer the frame for understanding the consequences operating inside you. As an instance, nobody is only a personality type 2. Two has a One-wing or perhaps a Three-wing, and also both's Management of Disintegration (Eight) and its own Management of Integration (Four) play crucial roles in her or his general personality.

Fundamentally, the objective is for all us to "go " the Enneagram, including exactly what each type signifies and acquiring the nutritious abilities of every one of types. The perfect is to develop into balanced, fully functioning one who are able to draw the power (or by the Latin, "merit") of every asneeded. Every one of those kinds of the Enneagram signifies different crucial elements of what we will need to attain this ending. The style type we begin life together is less crucial fundamentally than how well (or poorly) we utilize our type because first point for the Self Development and self-realization.

The 3 Instincts

The 3 Instincts (often wrongly called "that the Sub-types") really are a third-party pair of distinctions which are very vital for understanding personality. An important facet of human nature is located inside our instinctual "hard wiring" as aliens. We all are well endowed with special instinctual intelligences which are required to the survival as individuals and as a species. We all possess a self-preservation instinct (for maintaining the human body and its own life and functioning), a sexual urge (for stretching in the surroundings and throughout the generations), and also a societal instinct (so you can get along with the others and forming stable social bonds).

While we've three Instincts on us one of these is that the Dominant focus of the attention and behavior --that the collection of values and attitudes which we have been attracted to and confident with. We all have another Instinct that's utilized to encourage both the dominant Instinct, together with a 3rd Instinct that's minimal developed--a true blind spot within our nature and our worth. That Instinct is at every one of those 3 places--many, mid, and developed--produces that which we call our own "Instinctual Stack" (just like a three-layer cake) together with your dominant Instinct on top, the following most developed Instinct at the center, and also minimal developed at the base).

These instinctual drives profoundly affect our Personalities, and also at exactly the exact same period, our characters largely determine how every person prioritizes these instinctual wants. So, while every individual being has three of the instincts operating in them personality causes us to be concerned with these instincts compared to another two. We predict that this particular instinct that our dominant instinct. This is inclined to become our primary priority--that the subject of life we attend first. However, as soon as we're more swept up from the defenses of our personality--farther down the Degrees of Development-- our personality nearly all interferes together with all our dominant instinct.

Further our Enneagram kind tastes the way in that we Strategy our prominent instinctual need. Joining our Enneagram type together with your outstanding instinct gives an infinitely more special picture of the joys of the personality. As soon as we employ the distinctions of those 3 winners into the nine Enneagram types, they make 27 specific mixes of dominant and type instinct that consideration fully for gaps and variability over these types. We predict those mixtures that the Instinctual Variants.

The Enneagram Institute® Delivers an Internet test, the Instinctual Variants Questionnaire (IVQ), for assisting individuals decide not just Their instinct that is dominant, but in addition their Instinctual Stack. The IVQ additionally Provides a thorough personality profile based from the blend of this Test taker's Enneagram type, wing, and Instinctual Stack.

Listed below Are Some brief descriptions of the three instincts:

Self-preservation Instinct

Individuals that have this because their instinct that is dominant are. Obsessed with the safety, relaxation, health, energy, and also wellbeing of their body. In a wordthey have been concerned about using enough tools to satisfy life's requirements. Identification with your system is an essential attention for most humans, and also we want the own body to work well to be able to become more living and active at the globe. A lot of people in contemporary cultures never have faced death or life "survival" in the most basic sense; ergo, self-preservation types are inclined to get worried about food, money, home, health matters, and physiological relaxation. Moreover, those largely centered on self-preservation, by expansion, usually are interested in preserving those tools for many others too. Their attention of attention goes towards matters associated with those areas such as clothes, fever, decorating, shopping, and so on, especially if they're unsatisfied at these areas or possess an atmosphere of lack because of their childhoods. Self-Pres types are somewhat grounded, practical, acute, and more compared to another instinctual types. They may have busy social lives and also a fulfilling romantic relationship, however, should they believe their self-preservation needs aren't being fulfilled, but still do not be more happy or at ease. Inside their main relationships, this type of person "nesters"--they search national tranquility and security using a reliable, dependable partner.

Gender (aka"Attraction") Instinct

A Lot of People initially identify themselves since this kind as they've discovered the anal kinds are enthusiastic about"oneonone connections " However, all 3 instinctual kinds are enthusiastic about one of relationships for various reasons, therefore this will not distinguish them. The vital aspect in Gender types is the intense drive for stimulation and also a consistent understanding of this "chemistry" between others and themselves. Sexual kinds are instantly conscious of the appeal, or lack there of, between themselves as well as other individuals. Further, even whilst the cornerstone of the instinct is associated with novelty, it isn't fundamentally about people participating in the sexual activity. There are various individuals who individuals have been eager to be accessible for reasons of chemistry which we don't have any intention of "becoming associated " Yet we may possibly be mindful that individuals feel aroused using people's company and less so than the others. The sensual type is perpetually moving toward this feeling of intense stimulation and succulent energy inside their own relationships and in their own activities. They truly are probably the very "energized" of those 3 instinctual types, and also have a tendency to be aggressive, competitive, energized, and more emotionally intense compared to the Self-Pres or even societal types. Sexual types will need to own intense lively control within their principal relationships, or they stay frustrated. They like being deeply involved--merged-- along with the others, also certainly will eventually become disenchanted with spouses that cannot fulfill their dependence on intense lively union. Losing yourself at a "combination" to be would be your perfect here, and Sexual kinds are ever searching for this particular nation along with the others with stimulating items on the planet.

Societal (aka"Flexible") Instinct

As a Lot of People tend to misidentify themselves Sex classes because they desire One on One connections, many Men and Women neglect to Recognize themselves as Social types due to the fact that they obtain the (false) idea that This means constantly being included with classes, meetings, and parties. In case Self-preservation forms are interested in correcting the surroundings to create Themselves comfortable and secure, Social Type-S accommodate themselves to Serve the demands of their societal situation they end up. Ergo, Social forms are tremendously aware of others, whether they're in Intimate scenarios or in classes. They're Also Conscious of the way their activities and Approaches are impacting people around them. Additionally, anal kinds seek Proximity, Social types seek personal connection: they would like to remain in Long-term connection people also to participate with their world. Social Type S Will be the most worried about doing things which is going to have some effect in the Community, and on occasion even wider domain names. They tend to be warmer, more receptive, Engaging, and socially in relation to the other two types. Inside their main Relationships, they search mates with whom they are able to share societal tasks, desiring their intimates to become associated with events and projects together with them. Ironically, they really tend to prevent long periods of private familiarity and silent privacy, watching both as potentially limiting. Social forms lose Their awareness of individuality and significance once they're not a part of the others in Activities that surpass their unique interests.

Where does the enneagram come from?

The foundation of the start of the enneagram is indefinite. Ancient pioneers in its own evolution maintained, without solid evidence, to have heard its notions from early arcane customs, just to later take hedge or back their own words. A few sometimes maintained and sometimes refused creativity. Some were cagey in their origins and affects. Form your own decisions as, read about the ancient history of this enneagram, you fall upon ambiguities.

Also known in our period, the enneagram began with George Gurdjieff.

The Upcoming Big figure from the Development of this enneagram of character was siphoned Oscar Ichazo (born 1931).

The Internet article "Buenos Aires Mystery School? Oscar Ichazo, Arica and Castaneda" from Corey Donovan quotations from the 1973 meeting with Ichazo printed in the 1982 Arica Institute book Interviews with Oscar Ichazo. In summary, Ichazo reported he was 19, he met with a person in La Paz, Bolivia who was simply at a tiny set in Buenos Aires, Argentina who studied such understanding raising methods since the Gurdjieff work, the Kaballah, Sufism, and Zen Buddhism. The band mentored Ichazo for over a couple of decades after which helped him to travel into the East to study such customs like yoga, Buddhism, Confucianism, and I Ching. I haven't yet discovered alliance of this narrative.

Decades later Ichazo discussed these as well as other ancient changes in his "Letter to the Transpersonal Community." (Notice: Until recently, this correspondence has been offered at the Arica Institute internet site webpage, under Articles. Today I Can't get into the Arica Institute Site. The connection I have given will be on a replica of this "Letter" at the Scribd site.)

From the "Twist..." Ichazo Disparages the creativity of Gurdjieff's teachings, finding them to become universal theories taught in early Hindu scriptures, by the Magi, by philosophers of early Greece, etc. He cautioned that Gurdjieff generated the enneagram symbol displayed by Ouspensky, saying an enneagram was clearly one of those 'seals' of Pythagoras. I haven't yet found encouraging evidence for or against Ichazo's assert that Gurdjieff failed to considerably influence that he (Ichazo) heard the enneagram out of Pythagoras, perhaps not Gurdjieff. I'm still on the lookout for a very clear image of a Pythagorean enneagram.

From the "Letter...", Ichazo explained that which their very own initial contributions were on the maturation of the enneagram and celebrated his own applications of their enneagram. He voiced admiration that Claudio Naranjo educated what he learned out of Ichazo accurately with due credit.

Protoanalysis and Enneagrams

From his research and ponderings, Ichazo developed something of theories and clinics he called Protoanalysis. From 1956, study groups met major Latin American cities to master and also talk Ichazo's thoughts. Back in 1968 Ichazo lectured on Protoanalysis at the Institute of Applied Psychology at Santiago, Chile. That Exact Same season, in Arica, Chile, Ichazo established the Arica School or Institute to instruct Protoanalysis to Choose pupils. Back in 1971 he transferred the faculty into the USA, initially to NYC. Now the Arica Institute internet site lists a program of set trainings in quite a few US states as well as other nations.

As a part of the Protoanalysis app, Ichazo developed more than one hundred enneagrams--that the enneagram emblem educated by Gurdjieff, using various collections of tags applied into the 9 points from Ichazo for unique purposes. 1 manner that Ichazo used the enneagram emblem was always to diagram his theory of two self-types, each having a distinguishing'fixation','snare','idea',''fire', and'merit'.

The dining table reveals Ichazo's English Language enneagram tags for your nine self-categories.

A good illustration is a character Type 9 (such as me) has been slothful (indolent(idle), which might manifest as day dreaming, being "spaced out", indulging in escapism(or even focusing upon busy-work and topics of little effect alternatively of priorities. A Sort 9 averts claiming his herself. Nines have a tendency to really feel unlovable therefore attempt to become unnoticed also to maintain everyone they encounter placated. Once they receive the concept that God's love comprises them, they are able to start to displace habitual sloth with effective actions.

From the early 1970s, Claudio Naranjo educated the enneagram into Helen Palmer, One of others. Harper Row printed Palmer's publication The Enneagram: Understanding Yourself and Others in Your Daily Life at 1988. Oscar Ichazo's Arica Institute sued Palmer for copyright infringement. The Arica Institute largely lost the situation. The situation is recorded in Arica Institute, Inc., Plaintiff-Appellant, v. Helen Palmer and also Harper & Row Publishers, Incorporated, Defendants-Appellees. No. 771, Docket 91-7859. United States Court of Appeals, Second Circuit. Argued Jan. 30, 1992. Decided July 22, 1992 . undefined

The estimate of the Second Circuit US Court of Appeals pointed out that just Original expression could be copyrighted, and this discovery of truth can't be copyrighted. He pointed out that the Arica School's very own books quotation Ichazo as saying he didn't invent or generate exactly the enneagram or the 'fixations', etc., but instead those were facts of nature he discovered. When it comes to law instance (and without suggesting any remark concerning whether the asserted facts come infact truth), the Court of Appeals judge (such as the initial judge) said he would simply take Ichazo in his sentence and described Ichazo could perhaps not with consequences both assert he had been teaching discovered untrue facts about nature and assert his own teachings had been copyrightable.

The judge confirmed, although neither an idea nor a Simple Fact is copyrightable, A first expression of a concept or of a simple fact is copyrightable, and he pointed out how a succession of advice is presented could or might not be copyrightable. Putting historical facts in chronological arrangement [such as, for example, to present my own, personal cases, a bare set of those emperors of ancient Rome or of the significant conflicts of World War I] would be copyrightable, as there's nothing creative such an inventory. Considering the fact that Arica books represented the arrangement of fixations being a pure fact, just like the rainbow color arrangement, and maybe not really a subjective option, it demonstrated that no imagination has been included with presenting that detected sequence. Nevertheless, the judge reasoned that Ichazo's putting the arrangement of this fixations of their two personality types as labels over the enneagram was original -- Gurdjieff's depictions of these enneagram hadn't any words -- also had been minimally creative, also there were still additional ways others might pose the arrangement, to ensure particular means of tagging the enneagram was copyrightable. But he consented with the initial estimate that Palmer's uses of copyrightable Arica substance were tolerable as"fair usage"

Even though Ichazo along with also his Arica School largely lost the Copyright-infringement Instance, the instance had favorable consequences. It placed on listing his function as in a few respects the discoverer as well as in certain respects the originator of this Enneagram of this Fixations, the Spirit of this Enneagram of Personality. The case ceased his seminal donations from being forgotten and ignored. By what I have read, many crucial, major works over the

Enneagram ever since have given due honor and credit into Gurdjieff, Ichazo, and Naranjo.

Still another consequence of this situation was to allow all from the entire world understand that anybody had the best to provide that the Enneagram of Personality their particular descriptions, interpretations, and improvements, or even to set the enneagram emblem itself into anything other intent.

Seeing the gaps between Ichazo and Palmer, visit too Ichazo's "Letter to the Transpersonal Community", mentioned previously from the Ichazo capsule.

Wing Types

The Tails are the Enneagram Mode Amounts of side of the Heart Enneagram style; at basic wing theory, 9 and two are wings for your; 3 and 1 are 2 wings for Twos; 4 and 2 are two wings for Threes; 5 and 3 are tails for Fours; 6 and 4 are wings for Five S; 5, 5 plus wings and

7 for Sixes; 8 and 6 are 5 tails for Sevens; 7 and 9 are horns for Eights; also 1 and 8 are 2 tails for Nines.

You can see this pattern around the Enneagram emblem, also this is among Lots of ways the Enneagram symbol gets to be a sign of self-understanding along with growth. Most educators of the Enneagram concur totally that wings exist and these wings add potential faculties to our heart Enneagram style. Wings tend not to affect your heart motivational or personality arrangement, however they don't explain why just two individuals of the similar style act slightly differently. Many Enneagram teachers think that an individual has just 1 wing and not many teachers state there aren't any wings at all for anybody however I'm of the fact people could have one wing, two limbs, or no strings in any way.

Who's the foundation is the origin reliable?

I presume, however, aren't sure, that wing concept originated with Oscar Ichazo or Claudio Naranjo.

Because Gurdjieff failed to give attention to the enneatypes as tangible amounts, it could follow the horns -- because we now know them would perhaps not have originated . As soon as I spent seven days using Claudio last summer in Germany, he'd cite horns on a couple of occasions, and also the very fascinating reference was that: Claudio reported that while you can find some Enneagram educators (he said no names) who genuinely believe that in the event you realize an individual's wing, then you are able to determine that each's sub-type, " he (Claudio) said he failed whatsoever believe that this goes wrong.

Can it be an authentic model or theory that explains some part of reality a lot better compared to other models?

It's Been my expertise using enormous numbers of people that Just about everybody who sees the Enneagram readily describes with one or limbs as a means to clarify themselves accurately and also to know the others. Oftentimes, individuals with whom I've worked to spot their Enneagram fashions usually do not relate with presenting a wing or wings, but those are the exceptions.

Can it be useful and practical; can it help us take action we cannot do as well with no?

Knowing the wings or wing of a person assists individuals Know why, as an instance, a Five with a Six wing exhibits distinct behavior compared to the usual Five with a double wing. A Five with a Six wing includes dual emotional energy -- both the Fives and Sixes are Emotional Center fashions -- so they have a tendency to be cautious and cerebral compared to the usual Five with a double wing wing. Because Fours are still an Emotional Heart or Heart Center style, Five S with Four limbs have a tendency to be emotional and possess, in a feeling, a dual perception of abandonment. Fives and Fours possess a common sense of jealousy, also that I heard somebody clarify Fours and Fives like this (and I wish I could remember the origin): Fours and Fives both feel left handed, however Fours know they will have been left handed and shout about this (so they have "wet" abandonment). In comparison, Five S have learned to dwell within this condition without a further shout (ergo, "tender" abandonment). A Five using a Six could still be described as a Five star, however he or she'd be deeply mental and analytical.

Wings will also be helpful for growth and development. Because Most people Have the capacity to get both Wings, in case we aren't obtaining the favorable qualities of both other fashions, we're overlooking a number of our chances for growth.

Notice: For all those of you curious in how to use your own Wings to get Growth, actions on how best exactly to achieve that come at The Enneagram advancement Guide. I generated this 300-page novel, that includes 50+ developmental tasks for each Enneagram style -- coordinated by type and by the areas by which individuals wish to cultivate -- to produce development more accessible for individuals, Enneagram teachers, and managers, and trainers. It's designed for $27 (USD) throughout my site.

Here's the basic details about the tails for each Enneagram style and the way that these wings reinforce our heart Enneagram fashions.

Wings for Your

Nine Wing: Ones with a left-wing possess a greater power to relax and unwind with no to carry on a break, are somewhat less responsive once they disagree with some body, and also therefore are much more inclined to solicit the comments of the others as opposed to relying chiefly in their particular conclusions or those others that they admire.

Two thirds: Ones using two wing are far more persistently Generous and people-focused, along with being a lot more prudent and showing consistent warmth into others.

Wings for Twos

One Wing: whenever Twos have usage of their own wing they also balance their attention on individuals who have a devotion to action, are somewhat more discerning about people and situations, pay more attention to detail, and also possess a heightened capacity to be business and also to say no, together with less stress about how the others are going to react in their mind whenever they maintain themselves this manner.

Three Wing: Twos using a 3 wing are a Lot More comfy Getting observable, like holding a high-profile leadership standing. Additionally, those Twos feel convenient admitting their want to succeed; in reality, they frequently pursue being respected just as far as being enjoyed.

Wings for Threes

Two thirds: Threes with 2 wings tend to be a lot more sensitive to the feelings of many others and much more generous with their resources and time, plus they frequently concentrate on helping the others within their own professional or individual lives.

Four thirds : Threes that own a 4 wing are far more in Experience of their particular feelings, are prepared to take part in emotional conversations along with the others, possess a deeper personal presence, and could take part in some sort of artistic reflection or elegant amount of artistic admiration.

Wings for Fours

Three Wing: whenever Fours have a 3 wing, they're more action oriented, so possess higher and more consistent energy , exhibit more poise and confidence, and also therefore are somewhat more confident with being exceptionally observable in the place of shying off from feeling or visibility ambivalent about that.

Five Wing: Fours using a five-star are far more goal and Analytical, which delivers a counter point for their subjective emotional method of seeing other people.

Additionally, they possess a heightened capacity to comprehend situations from the far more considered and less responsive view and frequently demonstrate more self-restraint and self-containment.

Wings for Five S

Four Wing: Five S with a 4 wing are somewhat more mentally expressive and sensitive and in addition have a decorative outlook, perhaps doing the arts themselves -- as an instance, writing poetry, books, or screenplays or being artists or photographers.

Six Wing: Five S using a Six wing highlight and participate longer Readily with groups, have a tendency to put increased significance on devotion, and might have enhanced intuitive in sight. Even though a number of different Five S may likewise be quite enlightening, their opinions are more out of putting facts together and participating in extensive analysis. When Fives have a wing, the insights come quicker whilst the product of processing.

Wings for Sixes

Five Wing: whenever Sixes have a five-star, they're more internally than externally focused and so are even more self-explanatory and controlled, hence tempering their propensity to be responsive. Additionally, they possess a heightened passion for comprehension and apply the quest for comprehension not merely to collect information so as to really feel prepared, but also for your pure joy of studying.

Seven Wing: It can be stated that Sixes watch that the glass Half vacant and Sevens watch it as half full. So, when Sixes have a two-wing wing, they view the whole glass and so are usually cheerful, not as stressed, more positive, and higher-energy.

Wings for Sevens

Six Wing: Sevens with a right-wing add the capacity to know situations like being half-full and half-empty. As these Sevens possess a greater perceptiveness and also an ability to anticipate likely issues, their activities be much more deliberate and less predicated in their immediate responses.

Eight Wing: Sevens having an Eight wing Are Inclined to be Direct, assertive, and more successful. They've an even far more grounded presence and also a heightened desire to place thoughts in actions.

Wings for Eights

Seven Wing: Eights with a left-wing incorporate a light heartedness into the usually more severe Eight standpoint, are somewhat more high-spirited and separate, and are inclined to be a lot more daring and ready to try new items within their professional lifestyles with regard to experimentation and fun.

Nine Wing: Eights using a left-wing are interpersonally Warmer, more serene, and not as responsive, plus so they solicit and pay attention to the others' opinions as they tend to be more consensually oriented.

Wings for Nines

Eight Wing: Nines having an Eight wing possess a more take-charge Orientation, displaying a solidity and forcefulness whilst still Keeping up an urge to know the others' comments. With a Very Good Eight Wing, Nines maintain their particular points of perspective readily and also make fast and clear conclusions, even at the face of strong resistance.

CHAPTER TWO

THE NINE PERSONALITY TYPES

The Enneagram has Its Own Origins from the world's great spiritual Customs as well as in Pythagorean math --that implies to me this system meets our fundamental human faculties and cognitive requirements. We want the viewpoints and talents of several kinds of visitors to simply help our exceptionally intelligent and societal websites survive.

Exactly what Provides Enneagram its clinical usefulness in the consulting room has been its own attention to the largely unconscious core beliefs which shape people's perspective of just how to lead a life that is satisfying. As stated by Enneagram understandings our inherent core beliefs shape our focus of attention (at Enneagram terms "habit of mind") and we guide our energy ("the driving emotion of type"). Every one of those nine Enneagram types includes a different elastic pattern predicated up on and encouraging that a particular heart view, yet no type has been viewed as less or more healthy compared to every type. Listed below are short descriptions of the two fundamental kinds:

Type One: The Perfectionist, and also the Reformer considers you have to be good and appropriate to guarantee a fulfilling lifestyle in a World that needs good behaviour and punishes bad behaviour. Thus, Perfectionists are more diligent, responsible, improvement-oriented, and self-controlled, but could be very critical, resentful, and self-judging. In Accordance with The Enneagram Institute, both reformers are equally logical and idealistic, and also heart Faculties include being principled, purposeful, self-regulated, and also a perfectionist." [Reformers are both] conscientious and ethical, with a powerful awareness of wrong and right," '' The Enneagram Institute said. "They are teachers, crusaders, and advocates for change: always trying to improve matters, but afraid of making an error "

Ones are conscientious and ethical, with a solid awareness of Wrong and right. They're teachers, crusaders, and advocates for change: always trying to improve matters, but afraid of making a blunder. Well-organized, systematic, and fastidious, they strive to manage high standards, but can slip into being critical and perfectionistic. They routinely have problems with resentment and impatience. In their best: clever, discerning, realistic, and noble. May be quite epic.

· Fundamental Stress: to Be corrupt/evil, faulty

· Fundamental Wish: To be good, to have integrity, to become balanced

· Enneagram One using a Nine-Wing: "The Idealist"

· Enneagram One using a Two-Wing: "The Advocate"

Key Motivations: Wish To be appropriate, to attempt higher and enhance everything, to be in keeping with their beliefs, to justify themselves to be outside criticism as never to be convicted by anybody.

The Significance of this Arrows (in short)

When going into their Management of Disintegration (anxiety), Methodical Ones unexpectedly become moody and ridiculous in Four. But when moving into their Management of Integration (growth), mad, critical Ones be much impulsive and happy, such as healthy Sevens.

History is filled with Ones who've abandoned comfy lives to Do something outstanding since they believed that something high was calling them. Throughout the 2nd World War, Raoul Wallenburg abandoned a Cozy Middle Class lifetime to function for its security of tens of thousands of European Jews from invading Nazis. Back in India, Gandhi left his wife and family and friends as a prosperous lawyer to eventually become an itinerant urge of Indian liberty and non-violent societal alterations. Joan of Arc abandoned her village in France to restore the throne into the Dauphin and also to divert the English out of the Nation. The idealism of each and every one of those Ones has prompted countless.

Ones are individuals of sensible actions --that they Want to become helpful at the best awareness of this word. But on some degree of consciousness they believe they"have a mission" to meet life, if just to decide to try their very best to lessen the disease that they view in their own environment.

Even though Ones-have a solid sense of function, in addition they an average of believe they must justify their actions to themselves, and usually to the others too. This orientation induces Ones to devote a whole lot of time considering the outcome of their activities, in addition to about how to save yourself from behaving against their own convictions. As a result of the, Ones frequently convince themselves they truly are "mind" type s, rationalists who move only on logic and objective reality. However, the actual film is slightly different: Ones are activists that are looking for a decent motive for the things they believe they need to do. They're folks of passion and instinct using convictions and conclusions to restrain and guide their activities.

From the attempt to stay true to their fundamentals, Ones withstand Being influenced with their instinctual drives, knowingly perhaps not committing for them expressing them too publicly. The outcome is actually a personality type that's issues with repression, immunity, and aggression. They're normally seen by the others because exceptionally self- regulated, even inflexible, even though this is simply not the way Ones adventure themselves. This indicates for them that they're sitting to a cauldron of fires and wants, and they'd improved "keep the lid " faking they and everybody around them repent it.

Ones Think that being rigorous together (and finally Becoming "perfect") will warrant them in their eyes and in the eyes of the others. However, by trying to generate their particular new devotion, they frequently make their personal hell. Rather than agreeing with the statement in Genesis that God saw what He had established, "plus it had been fine," Ones intensely believe that "It was not --that there have been any mistakes!" This orientation helps make it hard for people to trust that their inner guidance--really, to trust lifetime so Ones come to rely heavily upon their super ego, a heard voice in their own youth, to direct them "the greater good" they thus passionately seek. When Ones are becoming completely entranced within their style, there's not much differentiation between them and also this intense, unkind voice. Separating out of this and seeing its own strengths and limits will be exactly what growth for your is approximately.

Type One--Quantities of Development

Healthy Degrees

Measure inch (In Their Finest): Become incredibly wise and discerning. By accepting exactly what Is, they get transcendentally realistic, and knowing that the very best actions to take in each moment. Humane, inspirational, and hopeful: that the facts are going to soon be heard.

Level-2: Conscientious With powerful personal histories: they've got a rigorous awareness of right and wrong, personal spiritual and ethical worth. Need to be fair, honest, self-disciplined, older, medium whatsoever.

Amount 3: Unbelievably Principled, always wish to be reasonable, objective, and ethical: justice and truth chief worth. Awareness of responsibility, personal ethics, as well as a greater purpose frequently make sure they are witnesses and teachers to the reality.

Average Degrees

Measure 4: Dis-satisfied with fact, they get high-minded idealists, believing it is all up for them to boost everything: crusaders, urges, critics. In to "causes" and trying to explain to others the way things "ought" to be.

Measure 5: Afraid Of building an error: what has to be in line with their own ideals. Become orderly and well-organized, however impartial, puritanical, emotionally constricted, rigidly keeping their feelings and instincts under control. Frequently workaholics--"anal-compulsive," punctual, pedantic, and so forth.

Amount 6: Highly Critical both of others and self: picky, judgmental, perfectionistic. Very opinionated about what: adjusting people and badgering them to"do the ideal thing"--since they visit it. Impatient never happy with anything unless it's done based on their own prescriptions. Moralizing, scolding, abrasive, and indignantly mad.

Allergic Levels

Amount 7: Could Be highly dogmatic, self-righteous, tender, and rigid. Begin working in absolutes: they know "the facts " Everyone is wrong: very acute in conclusions, while rationalizing particular activities.

Flat 8: Become Fanatical about imperfection and the wrongdoing of the others, even though they may possibly encounter conflicting activities, hypocritically doing precisely the contrary of what they preach.

Amount 9: Grow Condemnatory supporting the others, punitive and unkind to rid themselves of wrong doers. Intense depressions, nervous breakdowns, and suicide attempts are more likely. Generally, corresponds to this Obsessive-compulsive and Depressive character disorders.

Compatibility with Different Type S

Type-1 in connection with kind:

Inch Two 34 5 6789

Misidentification with Different Type S

Type Inch contrasted with kind:

Two 3456789

Addictions

Excessive utilization of vitamins, diets, and cleansing methods (fasts, diet pills, enemas). Under-eating for self-control: in most extreme cases anorexia and bulimia. Alcohol to alleviate tension.

Personal Growth Tips

For Enneagram Type Ones

· Learn How to unwind. Just take the time for yourself, without believing which what is your choice or what you don't accomplish will lead to turmoil and tragedy. Mercifully, the remainder of this world doesn't rely on you, despite the fact that you could sometimes feel it will.

· You've got a whole lot to instruct the others and are a fantastic teacher, but don't expect the others to shift instantly. What's obvious to you may possibly perhaps not be obvious to these, especially if they aren't utilized to become self-disciplined and intent on themselves because you're on your own. Lots of folks could also wish to accomplish what's right and might agree with you in principle however also for a variety of reasons simply aren't able to change straight away. The simple fact that many others usually do not change instantly according to your own prescriptions doesn't signify they won't change sometime later on. Your voice above all, your case may possibly do better than you are aware, even though they could take more than you expect. Therefore, have patience.

· It's not hard that you wind into a lather about the wrong doings of the others. Plus, it could at times be true which they're incorrect. However, what could it be for you personally? Your aggravation using them is going to do nothing to help them determine the following way to be. In the same way, avoid your persistent aggravation with your "short comings." Can your very own unpleasant self-criticism genuinely allow one to improve? Or does this only cause you to be stressed, nervous, and also self-doubting? Learn how to comprehend the strikes of one's super-ego and also the way in which they undermine as opposed to allow you to.

· It's essential that you get in touch with your feelings, especially your subconscious impulses. You might discover that you're uncomfortable with your emotions as well as your sexual and aggressive instincts --in summary, with all the cluttered individual things which make us human anatomy. It may be good for maintain a diary or to enter into some type of group therapy or alternative band work both to build up your own feelings and also to observe others won't condemn you to having individual requirements and limits.

· Your Achilles' heels are the selfrighteous anger. You get mad easily and so are confounded by what appears to one to truly be the most bizarre refusal of the others to get the ideal thing--since you've identified it. Attempt to step down and understand your anger wracking folks therefore they can't hear lots of the excellent stuff you need to state. Further, your repressed anger could be providing you with an ulcer or higher blood pressure also is just a harbinger of worse things ahead.

Type 2: The Giver, or even Helpers considers You Have to give entirely to others to guarantee a fulfilling lifestyle Within a give-to-get universe. Thus, Givers are affectionate, friendly, encouraging, and relationship-oriented, but could be prideful, too sensitive, and rigorous. In the event that you always put other people's wants and needs in front of one's own, you may possibly be described as a helper. The Enneagram Institute noticed that helpers are generous, caring, demonstrative, and tend to be equally individuals' pleasers and possessive." [Helpers] are more friendly, generous, and self-sacrificing, but may also be sentimental, flattering, and people-pleasing. They truly are well-meaning and motivated to be near the others but can slip into doing things for the others so as to become needed. They routinely have problems with possessiveness and with acknowledging their own preferences."

Twos are empathetic, sincere, and warm-hearted. They're Friendly, generous, and self-sacrificing, but may also be sentimental, flattering, and people-pleasing. They truly are well-meaning and motivated to be near the others but can slip into doing things for the others as a way to become needed. They routinely have problems with possessiveness and with acknowledging their own preferences. In their very best: unselfish and altruistic, they have unconditional love to the others.

· Fundamental Stress: to Be undesirable, unworthy of being adored

· Fundamental Wish: To feel adored

· Enneagram Two having a One-Wing: "Servant"

· Enneagram Two having a Three-Wing: "The Host/Hostess"

Key Motivations: Wish To be adored, to state their own feelings for many others, to be wanted and valued, for other people to react to them to vindicate their claims about themselves.

The Significance of this Arrows (in short)

When going into their Management of Disintegration (anxiety), Needy Twos unexpectedly become competitive and dominating in eight. But when moving into their Management of Integration (growth), prideful, self-deceptive Twos be much more self-nurturing and mentally aware, such as healthy Fours.

Getting generous and moving out of the way of many others makes Twos believe that theirs would be the wealthiest, most meaningful way to call home. The love and anxiety that they believe --and also the actual great they perform --ignites their hearts and also leaves them feel rewarding. Twos are interested in what they believe to function as "really, very good" things in life including love, proximity, sharing, family, and friendship.

If Twos are more healthy and in equilibrium, they're Adoring, friendly, generous, and considerate. Individuals are interested in them like bees to honey. Healthy Twos warm the others at the shine of their own hearts. They enliven the others with their own attention and appreciation, helping individuals to see favourable qualities in themselves they had not previously realized. Simply speaking, healthy Twos would be the embodiment of all "the fantastic parent" that everybody else wants they'd: somebody who sees them since they're, knows them together with immense empathy, helps and promotes infinite patience, and so is always eager to give a hand while knowing the way in which and when to go. Healthy Twos open our hearts as theirs are so receptive and also they reveal how to become deeply and deeply human.

But Twos' internal development could be restricted by their own "shadow side"--pride, Self-Deception, the propensity to develop into over-involved from the lifestyles of many others, and also the inclination to control others to acquire their very own psychological needs fulfilled. Transformational work involves moving into shadowy regions within ourselves, and also this quite definitely goes against the grain of their two's character arrangement, that prefers to see in only the very favourable, luminous terms.

Perhaps the biggest barrier facing Twos, Threes, and Fours In their internal work is needing to handle their inherent Center concern with worthlessness. Underneath the outside, three types fear which they are without value independently, and thus they need to do something outstanding so as to win love and approval by the others. From the typical to Bad Levels, Twos pose a false image to be utterly liberal and unselfish and not needing any sort of payoff to themselves, even when in actuality they are able to have enormous expectations along with unacknowledged mental needs.

Typical to Bad Twos Seek approval of their values by minding their super-ego's requirements to sacrifice themselves . They believe they must always put others and become loving and unselfish should they wish to find love. The issue is that "putting the others " leaves Twos covertly mad and resentful, emotions that they work hard to repress or reject. But they finally erupt in a variety of manners, interrupting Twos' connections and showing that the inauthenticity of how lots of the ordinary to poor Two's claims regarding the thickness of these "love"

Type 2 --Quantities of Development

Healthy Degrees

Degree Inch (In Their Most Useful): Become Deeply unselfish, humble, and altruistic: giving unconditional love for others and self. Feel it's really a privilege to stay the lifestyles of many others.

Level-2: Empathetic, Compassionate, feeling like others. Caring and worried with their demands. Thoughtful, warm-hearted, forgiving and true.

Degree 3: Encourages And respectful, capable to find that the good in the others. Service is essential, but protects self: they have been still nurturing, generous, and giving a truly loving individual.

Average Degrees

Degree 4: Desire to function as Closer to the others, therefore start "individuals satisfying," becoming too friendly, emotionally demonstrative, and also packed with "good intentions" around what. Give enchanting care: approval, "strokes," flattery. Love is the ultimate price, plus so they discuss this constantly.

Measure 5: Become too Intimate and intrusive: they have to be needed; therefore they put, meddle, and get a handle on in the name of romance. Wish others to rely upon them give, however hope that a return send dual messages. Enveloping and possessive: the co-dependent, self-sacrificial man who may not perform enough for many others --wearing out themselves for everyone, causing needs to allow them to satisfy.

Measure 6: More Self-important and self-satisfied, believe that they have been crucial, even though they over rate their efforts from the others' behalf. Hypochondria, learning to be a "martyr" others. Over-bearing, patronizing, presumptuous.

Allergic Levels

Degree 7: Could be Manipulative and self-serving, instilling guilt by telling the others how much that they owe them and cause them to suffer. Abuse food and drugs to "stuff feelings" and obtain empathy. Undermine people, which makes belittling, disparaging opinions. Unbelievably self-deceptive concerning their motives and aggressive or covetous their behaviour is.

Amount 8: Domineering And coercive: texture qualified to get whatever that they desire from the others: that the repayment of old debts, cash, and sexual favours.

Amount 9: Willing to explanation and reevaluate the things they do given that they are feeling mistreated and victimized by the others And are angry and resentful. Somatization in Their aggression's outcomes In chronic health issues since they vindicate themselves from "falling Apart" and burdening the others. Generally, corresponds to this Histrionic Personality Infection and Factitious Illness.

Addictions

Abusing over the counter and food medications. Bingeing, notably on candies and carbs. Overeating from atmosphere"love-starved;" in extreme cases caked. Hypochondria to start looking for compassion.

Personal Development Tips

For Enneagram Type Twos

· First of all, bear in mind that in case you aren't fixing your needs, it's exceedingly improbable you will have the ability to meet anybody else needs without issues, inherent resentments, along with continual frustration. Further, you won't be as able to react to people in a balanced manner when you haven't gotten sufficient rest, also cared for yourself precisely. It's not egotistical to ensure you are ok before replying others' needs--it's only good sense.

· Attempt to be much more alert to your own personal motives once you opt to assist someone. While doing good stuff for people is surely a decent attribute, whenever you achieve this as you expect that the other person to love you personally or perform something nice for you in exchange, you're setting yourself up for disappointments. Your type comes with a true threat of slipping in to subconscious co-dependent patterns together with family members, plus so they never bring you exactly what you really desire.

· When there are lots of things which you may wish to accomplish to folks, it's frequently much better to inquire exactly what they really need. You're talented at accurately intuiting the others' feelings and preferences, but this doesn't necessarily signify they desire those demands adjusted by you personally in the manner in which you are thinking about. Communicate your aims, and become eager to accept a "no thankyou." Somebody deciding they don't want your distinct offer of help doesn't follow they dislike you personally or are depriving you.

· Fight the desire to listen to your own good works. As soon as you've done something like the others, don't remind them. Allow it to be either they are going to remember your kindness and invite you inside their particular manner or else they won't. Your calling awareness of exactly what you did for these just sets people on the area and causes them to feel uncomfortable. It won't meet anybody or increase your connections.

· Learn how to comprehend the affection and good wishes of the others, even though those are maybe not in relation that you're knowledgeable about. While others might not state their own feelings in a sense which you simply want, they are helping you discover in additional manners simply how much they worry for you. In the event that it's possible to comprehend what the others are giving you, then you will break easier in the data that you are adored. Love is available but just to the level that we're present and so are open to it.

Type Three: Your Performer considers You Have to reach and triumph to guarantee that a fulfilling lifestyle in a universe that rewards doing, in the place of simply being. Thus, Performers are industrious, fast paced, goal-focused, and efficiency-oriented, but could be inattentive into feelings, impatient, and image-driven.

Enneagram Threes will appreciate achievement and desire to Function as ideal. Because of this, efficacy, results, image and recognition are essential for them.

Threes attempt for success within their chosen field and are normally highly flexible and prepared to accommodate to realize their targets. In their finest, the others are going to experience Threes overly hardworking, principled and open minded, offering the gifts of integrity and hope into the globe. Within an unhealthy condition, the Three's over-expressed demand for achievement might appear self-important and inconstant. This comes from a feeling of self-worth that's developed on what exactly the Three will, as opposed to that which they have been.

The presents of this Enneagram Three comprise:

· Ambition: Threes are tough and have the energy and will to make an effort to become the best in anything they choose on. They rely on their capacity to ensure success.

· Successful: The three knows the way to accomplish things in a means that's productive and efficient.

· Flexible: Together with being willing to accommodate to realize their objectives, Threes can conform to unique conditions, people or surroundings skilfully.

· Driven: The Three's top energy and excitement for endeavours has things done and compels the others to carry out also.

· Results-Oriented: Placing targets and employing themselves to attain those are natural to Threes as breathing. They're centered on the end-result.

Average Action Patterns:

As a "doer" and also Goaldirected kind, Threes Concentrate on the Task in the hand and also are active in working towards their own targets. The elastic Three is frequently known as the "chameleon" since they change their character and accommodate their role, behaviour, communication and demonstration to accommodate the audience they want to impress. The validity of this Three will soon arrive at the fore on the job as well as in recreational pursuits. Some Threes are extremely attracted to tasks that permit human achievement and competition, while more societal Threes are attracted to winning teams. At a team atmosphere, the Threes can be attracted to leadership functions as well as many others will likely have them very energetic and optimistic. They dress for success and also is likely to be certain the way that they look serves their own purpose, audience and aspirations.

Average Thinking Patterns:

Threes Could Be very proficient at framing errors and Failures as "learning opportunities", letting them quickly proceed from those failures as opposed to residing in it and carrying the reverses personally. They discover that it's simple to get in touch with data that supports their perspective, while other advice will immediately disappear off. Being a calculating human, the Three's emotional energy is dedicated to their own targets and what is necessary to reach them. Their thought processes are inclined to become quick, permitting them to conform to changing scenarios instantly. Threes usually "check" or browse the specific situation to make sure they are behaving, engaging and communication in a means which may improve the possibilities of succeeding. The Three's validity is connected for their custom of emotionally comparing themselves to the others, resulting in feelings to be a lot better than or worse than some others. Threes have a tendency to over-identify together with their job, whether that job is corporate, creative or parenting, to this idea what they do defines who they truly are.

Average Feeling Patterns:

Threes are great at detaching in their feelings, to Prevent feelings getting in the method of success. They want to put emotions aside and certainly will seldom possess some moment for self-reflection or referring to feelings, especially opinions that are relevant solely to stress, depression and anxiety. While gloomy and stressed feelings are found in the Planet, that they think it is a lot easier to connect with anger and frustration. Threes are reluctant to risk that the fantastic opinion of powerful people therefore if individuals involved are fundamental to victory, the Three will likely fight to fully connect with those frustrations. A whole lot of a Three's sense facility will concentrate on what other men and women are responding to them. Their assurance is projected reluctantly, but inside Threes could be sense more cynical compared to their favourable behaviour shows to other folks. Projecting confidence is quite crucial that you Threes, that would like to appear positive and certainly will conceal feelings which could detract using the particular image. The others are so very likely to undergo Threes as unmoved, focused as well as marginally severe. Under repeated pressure or if up against the chance of failure, Threes are, nevertheless, prone to be much more short-tempered and eloquent.

Blind Spots

· Threes are extremely mindful of demonstration and graphic, which may get self-deceptive whenever they start thinking their own PR. In over-identifying together with their public image, Threes may possibly shed touch with that they're and make confusion between the actual self along with their occupation or function on the planet. The others might also tune in to it, inducing Threes as insincere, opportunistic as well as gallop.

· The Three finds it tough to explore negative dilemmas and certainly will frequently rush or ignore such discussions. This is going to be especially true when the criticism points involving shortcomings and mistakes.

· Strong goal-orientation and induce may possibly result in the others undergoing the Three as egocentric, hurried and dismissive -- behaviours that are intensified once the Three is coping with people which can come around as eloquent and might create them "look bad".

· A three's assurance might be projected certainty. Sometime certainty readily appears to be a fantastic thing, it could appear dismissive of other viewpoints, so keeping people from a dialog. It could decrease their willingness to the Three's inputs, aims and aims.

Type Number: The Romantic considers You Have to Get the Longed-for comprehensive and exceptionally Idealized relationship or position to make sure a fulfilling lifestyle at a universe that otherwise will leave you. Thus, Romantics are idealistic, profoundly sense, empathetic, accurate to self-love, but could be striking, moody, and sometimes self-absorbed.

Enneagram Fours possess the inspirational have to Express their uniqueness and become true. Fours significance individualism and consequently, feelings, self-expression and purpose will probably be crucial for them. They have been rather romantic in your mind and love beauty and creating significance for themselves and also others. In their finest, Fours are advocated as painful and sensitive content. They supply the present of equanimity and credibility to the world. A healthier Four might feel misunderstood, but some experience them as both melancholic as well as gallop. This pattern stems from the Four's intense understanding of their wounds and flaws.

The presents of this Enneagram Four comprise:

· Self-aware: Fours have been conscious of their feelings and those of the others and work to know those emotions. This permits them to join profoundly.

· Goal Driven: Being dismissive about what's purpose and meaning pushes Fours to state their own private purpose and participation into the globe.

· Launched: Their creative and creative capability empowers Fours to offer exceptional saying to what things for them.

· Sensitive: Fours can re-evaluate what's missing and can dive in to the center of things. Their feeling-based instinct allows them to be more exceptionally attuned to the surroundings.

· Courage: Fours are not shy away from anguish and also the painful details of the mental universe, and this also gives them the guts to ask difficult questions.

Average Feeling Patterns:

Fours Are Extremely linked to feelings, either the own and The psychological undercurrents within their own environment. They have been normally very conscious of others feelings, and sometimes more than many others are. This type has a tendency to live and continue for their own emotions intensely among the others could find them deep and intense. Fours rely on researching the entire array of emotions, from happiness to profound sadness plus so they can shift between those emotions because their experiences and world shift. They resonate with feelings like reduction, sadness and bitterness, which might result in cycles of depression. Fours have a tendency to take life very badly and may gain from getting the light heartedness of these development to Seven.

Average Action Patterns:

Fours love delving deeply into their own life and enjoy discussing Deep adventures with other individuals. Many knowingly encourage ritual for a means of creating meaning within their own lives. Their hunt for symbolism, inspiration and significance may possibly create a powerful romance with artistic reflection or appreciation of their arts. If Fours are participated with dull or extra-curricular activities, they're very likely to come to feel disenchanted and defeated. Fours head to amazing lengths to discuss their feelings and feelings at a real manner and many loves telling personal stories. This might just be with a select number but might also be with a wider audience. Their conversations additionally have a substantial number of personal "I, I, mine, myself" language and also are targeted toward establishing connections with other individuals.

Average Thinking Patterns:

The type is characterised by a Feeling of deficiency and jealousy, dedicated to and wanting for that which exactly is overlooking within themselves or within their lifetimes. Fours are extremely proficient at internalising and presuming unwanted details regarding themselves. They truly are extremely likely to lose optimistic data. This internalisation of critical advice could make Fours exceptionally responsive to whatever which appears to imply something negative about these. Fours' personal feelings and feelings can prejudice their perspective of their truth, resulting in subjective as opposed to objective decision-making. They are inclined to trust their emotions and experiences above all else. Fours are extremely introspective and are inclined to get frustrated with the standard, everyday reality. They may possibly become broody from the thinking process and obtain lost in unwanted thought-patterns that hamper their self-esteem, which makes them to be known.

Blind Spots

· Fours wish to own deep and meaningful connections but may most likely behave in a way that reflect their have to feel very different, separate and special. This may possibly cause them to pull people pushing and close them away, especially if the Four feels frustrated or rejected. The web effect may possibly cause people withdrawing out of their store.

· Fours can additionally give attention to what exactly is missing, desiring exactly what they don't really possess and rejecting the things they've got. This shifting focus strengthens their feelings of lack of emotional sensitivity.

· Fours might possibly not know about the degree to which they self-reference in conversations. Though the Four really wants to draw people nearby doing this, the others might experience this as self-absorbed.

· This sort is very likely to be actuated if people do not fully finish a dialog or do not provide them with the time that they have been asking. Fours usually have that the need to keep on together with conversations when the others are now not thinking about talking an issue.

· In thinking others share their own taste to talking feelings and emotions along with seeking emotional closing, Fours can survive on this too far. This could result in the others undergoing the Four as too intense and dramatic.

Type Five: The Observer considers You Have to protect yourself from invasion to cover a Satisfying life in a universe which requires too much and gives not enough. Thus, Observers are self-sufficiency-seeking, non-demanding, analytic/thoughtful, and discreet, but could be withholding, detached, and too confidential.

Fives are alert, insightful, and inquisitive. They Can Concentrate and concentrate on developing complex ideas and techniques. Independent, innovative, and inventive, they can also become preoccupied with their thoughts and imaginary constructs. They are detached, yet high-strung and intense. They routinely have problems with eccentricity, nihilism, and isolation. In their Best: visionary pioneers, often before their period, and ready to find the world in a totally new method.

· Fundamental Stress: Being useless, helpless, or reluctant

· Fundamental Wish: In order competent and capable

· Enneagram Five with a Four-Wing: "The Iconoclast"

· Enneagram Five with a Six-Wing: "The Problem Solver"

Key Motivations: Wish To have knowledge, to comprehend that the surroundings, to have all figured out like an easy method of protecting yourself out of dangers by the surroundings.

The Significance of this Arrows (in short)

When going into their Management of Disintegration (anxiety), Detached Five S unexpectedly become hyperactive and sprinkled at Seven. But when Moving into their Management of Integration (growth), avaricious, detached Five S Become more self-explanatory and more critical, such as healthy Eights.

Type Five Summary

We've got Named personality kind Five the Investigator because, more than just about any type, Five S wish to figure out why things are just how they truly are. They would like to comprehend the way the world works, while it's the cosmos, the world, the vegetable, animal, or mineral kingdoms--or even the interior of their own imaginations. They have been always hunting, asking questions, and delving in to matters in thickness. They usually do not accept received remarks and doctrines, setting a strong desire to try the facts of the majority of assumptions such as themselves.

Behind Five S' constant search for comprehension have been profound insecurities in their capacity to work successfully in the globe. Five S believe they don't need the capability to accomplish things in addition to the others. But instead than participate with tasks which may fortify their confidence, Five S"have a step backwards" in their heads by which they are feeling more competent. Their view is that contrary to the protection of their heads they'll sooner or later determine how to accomplish things--and also yet one day re-join the whole world.

Five S Spend a great deal of time watching and contemplating--playing the noises of end or using a synthesizer, or even taking notes to those actions in an anthill in their rear yard. While they immerse themselves into their own observations, they start to internalize their expertise and gain an atmosphere of self-confidence. They are able to go out and play with a bit on the synthesizer or educate people exactly what they understand regarding rodents. They could also encounter exciting fresh info or create new creative mixes (playing a sheet of music based on records of water and wind). Once they get confirmation in these observations and hypotheses, or view others know their own job, it's a verification of these proficiency, and also this meets their Fundamental Desire. ("do you understand what you're discussing.")

Knowledge, Understanding, and comprehension are so highly appreciated by Five S, as their identity is made around "having thoughts" and being someone with something odd and more enlightening to mention. Because of this, Five S aren't interested in researching what's familiar as well as non-meat; rather, their attention has been attracted to the odd, the missed, the trick, the occult, the more eccentric, the brilliant, the "unthinkable." Investigating "unknown land"--knowing something which the others have no idea or establishing something which no body has experienced--allows Five S to own a niche for themselves which nobody else succeeds. They genuinely believe developing this niche could be your very best means they are able to attain confidence and independence.

So, for Their own safety and self-esteem, Five S will need to possess a minimum of a single area in that they will have a level of expertise which may let them feel competent and related to the globe. Five S think, "that I will seek out something I can do well, after which I am going to have the ability to satisfy with the challenges of everyday life. I, however, can not possess anything else distracting me getting whatsoever " They hence develop an extreme focus on anything they are able to master and come to feel protected. It might function as the environment of math, or even the area of roll and rock up, or even classical songs, or even car mechanics, or even terror and science fiction, or even some universe entirely created within their own imagination. Perhaps not all Five S are Ph.Ds. However, with respect to their own intellect and the tools available in their mind, they focus heavily on mastering something that's caught their attention.

To get Worse or better, the more locations that Five S research don't be determined by societal endorsement; really, if the others trust their thoughts too readily, Five S have a tendency to fear that their thoughts may possibly be overly traditional. History is packed with famous Five S who overturned accepted manners of doing or understanding matters (Darwin, Einstein, Nietzsche). A lot more Five S, nevertheless, have grown to be lost from the byzantine intricacies of their thought processes, becoming only bizarre and exceptionally isolated.

The Intense attention of Five S can hence cause remarkable discoveries and creations, however once the personality is much more fixated, in addition, it can make self-defeating issues. That is only because their focus on attention unknowingly serves to divert them out of their pressing technical issues. No matter the sources in their anxieties can function --customs, absence of bodily strength, inability to acquire employment, etc --ordinary Fives usually do not address your difficulties. Rather they find another thing to do so which can cause them to feel much more competent. The stark reality is that irrespective of what amount of command that they develop within their field of expertise, this can't fix their basic insecurities regarding functioning on the planet. As an instance, like a marine biologist, a Five star might learn what there's to learn about a kind of shell fish, however in case her fear is that she's going to have the ability to conduct her household satisfactorily, she may not need solved her inherent anxiety.

Type Five--Quantities of Development

Healthy Degrees

Degree Inch (In Their Most Useful): Become visionaries, widely comprehending the World whilst penetrating it deeply. Openminded, simply take matters entirely, in their actual context. Get pioneering discoveries in order to find new methods of doing and perceiving things.

Measure 2: Observe everything with extraordinary perceptiveness and insight. Most mentally alert, curious, searching intelligence: nothing escapes their notice. Foresight and prediction. Able to concentrate become engrossed in what has caught their interest.

Measure 3: Attain skilful mastery of whatever interests. Excited by Knowledge: often become expert in a certain area. Innovative and inventive, producing extremely valuable, original works. Highly independent, idiosyncratic, and whimsical.

Average Degrees

Measure 4: Begin conceptualizing and Finetuning everything before behaving --functioning Things out of their heads: model construction, preparing, preparing, and collecting more funds. Studious, acquiring procedure. Be technical, and frequently "intellectual," frequently challenging accepted ways to do things.

Grade 5: wider detached as they are included with complex Thoughts or fanciful worlds. Become obsessed with their own dreams and interpretations instead of reality. Are fascinated with offbeat, esoteric themes, even those between black and troubling elements. Detached from the technical world, a "disembodied mind," even though high-strung and intense.

Measure 6: Start to have an antagonistic position toward whatever that would Hinder their inner environment and own vision. Become abrasive and provocative, with blatantly extreme and revolutionary viewpoints. Cynical and argumentative.

Allergic Levels

Degree 7: Grow and isolated in fact, bizarre and nihilistic. Highly unstable and fearful of aggressions: they both refuse and repulse all social attachments.

Degree 8: Get duped nonetheless fearful with their own threatening thoughts, getting Horrified, delirious victim to gross distortions and phobias.

Amount 9: Hunting oblivion, they can commit suicide or have a psychotic Break with fact. Deranged, explosively self-destructive, together with schizophrenic overtones. Generally, corresponds to this Schizoid Avoidant and Schizotypal personality disorders.

Addictions

Poor Sleeping and eating habits thanks to reducing demands. Neglecting nourishment and hygiene. Deficiency of physical exercise. Psychotropic medication for emotional stimulation and flow, narcotics such as stress.

Personal Development Tips

For Enneagram Form Five S

· Learn how to see whenever you're thinking and agreeing goes out of this immediacy of one's own experience. Your emotional abilities may be an outstanding gift, however, just may be a snare once you utilize these to escape from touch with others and yourself. Stay connected with your physicality.

· You are normally quite intense therefore high-strung that you will find it hard to relax and relax. Try an attempt to learn how to settle down into a healthful manner, without alcohol or drugs. Exercising or using biofeedback methods may help channel a portion of one's enormous nervous energy. Meditation, running, yoga, and dance are all especially beneficial for the own type.

· You see lots of chances but frequently don't know just how to select one of them judge that's less or more crucial. Whenever you're captured on your fixation, an awareness of view can be overlooking, and together with it the capability to produce accurate assessments.

At this time, it could be of assistance to find the recommendation of someone whose judgment you trust as you're gaining view in your own circumstance. Doing so could also assist you to anticipate someone else, an issue for the own type.

· Notice once you're getting intensely associated with endeavours which don't fundamentally encourage your self-esteem, confidence, or even life position. It's likely to trace many different interesting topics, games, games and pastimes, however they may get massive distractions out of what you understand you must do. Decisive actions may bring more confidence in learning more facts or acquiring greater conducive skills.

· Five S have a tendency to locate it hard to trust people, to start them up mentally to make them accessible in a variety of ways. Their comprehension of possible issues in relationships can often develop a self-fulfilling prophecy. It's crucial to not forget that having struggles with the others isn't odd and that the healthful factor is to use out them as opposed to deny attachments together with people by withdrawing to isolation. Having just one or two intimate friends whom you aspire to possess battles with will improve your own life significantly.

Personal Development tips

For Enneagram Type Five S

Learn how to see whenever you're thinking and thinking goes from this immediacy of one's adventure. Your emotional abilities may be an outstanding gift, however, just may be a snare once you utilize these to escape from touch with others and yourself. Stay connected with your physicality.

You are normally quite intense therefore high-strung that you will find it hard to relax and relax. Try an attempt to learn how to settle down into a healthful manner, without alcohol or drugs. Exercising or using biofeedback methods may help channel a portion of one's enormous nervous energy. Meditation, running, yoga, and dance are all especially beneficial for the own type.

You find lots of chances but frequently don't understand just how to select one of them judge that's less or more crucial. Whenever you're captured on your fixation, an awareness of view can be overlooking, and together with it the capability to produce accurate assessments. At this time, it could be of assistance to find the recommendation of someone whose judgment you trust as you're gaining view in your own circumstance. Doing so could also assist you to anticipate someone else, an issue for the own type.

Notice whenever you're getting intensely associated with endeavours which don't fundamentally encourage your self-esteem, confidence, or even life position. It's likely to trace numerous interesting topics, games, games and pastimes, however they may get massive distractions out of what you understand you must do. Decisive actions bring greater confidence in learning facts or acquiring more conducive skills.

Fives have a tendency to locate it hard to trust people, to start them up mentally to make them accessible in numerous ways. Their comprehension of possible issues in relationships can often develop a self-fulfilling prophecy. It's crucial to not forget that having struggles with the others isn't odd and that the healthful factor is to use out them as opposed to deny attachments together with people by withdrawing to isolation. Having just one or two intimate friends whom you aspire to possess battles with will improve your own life greatly.

Type Six: The Loyal Skeptic considers you must get certainty and security to both make sure a fulfilling lifestyle within a poisonous and erratic universe you cannot trust. Thus, Loyal Skeptics are trustworthy, curious, excellent friends, and coughing, but may be too cynical, accusatory and fearful.

The devoted, security-oriented type. Sixes are dependable, Hard-working, accountable, and reliable. Exemplary "trouble shooters," they exude issues and boost alliance, but could become more defensive, evasive, and anxious--working on anxiety whilst whining about any of it. They are sometimes attentive and indecisive, but also responsive, defiant and rebellious. They routinely have difficulties with self doubt and distress. In their very best: Emotionally stable and self-reliant, courageously championing others and themselves.

· Fundamental Stress: to Be with no assistance and advice

· Fundamental Wish: To possess support and security

· Enneagram Six using a Five-Wing: "The Defender"

· Enneagram Six using a Seven-Wing: "The Buddy"

Key Motivations: Wish To have safety, to feel encouraged by the others, to possess certitude and reassurance, to examine the attitudes of others, to fight anxiety and insecurity.

The Significance of this Arrows (in short)

When going into their Management of Disintegration (anxiety), Dutiful Sixes unexpectedly turn out to be competitive and haughty in Three. But when moving into their Management of Integration (growth), fearful, and hurtful Sixes be much relaxed and optimistic, such as healthful Ms.

Type Six Review

The motive Sixes are so faithful to other people is They Don't Want to get left and left with support--their Fundamental Stress. Ergo, the fundamental dilemma for type Six will be that a collapse of self-confidence. Sixes have come to feel they usually do not hold the interior tools to take care of life's challenges and vagaries independently, so increasingly count on allies, structures, beliefs, and also supports out for guidance to live. If acceptable structures usually do not exist, then they are going to help to create and maintain them.

Sixes would be the Principal kind from the Thinking Center, which suggests They've the most difficulty calling their own inner guidance. Consequently, they don't need faith in their minds and conclusions.

This doesn't follow they usually do not think. To the Contrary, they believe --and stress --a whole lot! In addition, they have a tendency to fear making major conclusions, but at precisely the exact same time they withstand with anybody make decisions on them. They would like to you shouldn't be commanded, but are likewise frightened of accepting responsibility in a means which may put them "at the type of flame " (The aged Japanese adage which says, "The blade of grass that grows excessive gets burnt off" pertains for the notion)

Sixes are always Conscious of the anxieties and therefore are constantly on the lookout for techniques to create "societal security" bulwarks against them. Should Sixes believe they will have up sufficient, they are able to proceed with a certain amount of confidence. However, should this crumble, they get stressed and self-doubting, then re-awakening their Fundamental Stress. ("I am in my very own! What am I really going to do today?") A fantastic question for Sixes may consequently be: "When can I know I have enough security?" Or, how to get into the center of this, "What's security?" Without Vital inner guidance and the profound awareness of service it attracts, Sixes are constantly fighting to find business ground.

Sixes Try to Construct a community of confidence over a desktop of unsteadiness and also fear. They're frequently full of a nameless stress and after that try to find or make explanations. Wanting to believe there is something solid and straightforward inside their own lives, they are able to be mounted on excuses or places that seem to spell out their own situation. Because "belief" (trust, faith, convictions, rankings) is problematic for Sixes to reach, and as it's essential for their feeling of equilibrium, as soon as they set a trusted belief, they don't readily question this, nor do they really desire the others to achieve that. The same goes for people within an Six's lifetime: once Sixes believe that they are able to expect some one, they're going to great lengths to keep up connections with the particular person who acts as a sounding board, a mentor, or even perhaps a ruler to the Six emotional reactions and behaviour. They consequently do everything within their capacity to maintain their affiliations going. ("Should I really don't trust, then I must find something within this universe I could expect.")

Type Six--Quantities of Development

Healthy Degrees

Degree Inch (In Their Most Useful): Become self-affirming, expecting of others and self, Independent however symbiotically interdependent and combined being the same. Belief itself contributes to authentic guts, positive thinking, direction, and rich self-expression.

Level-2: Able To elicit strong emotional responses from the others: very attractive, heterosexual, adorable, affectionate. Trust essential: bonding together with the others, forming permanent connections and alliances.

Measure 3: Dedicated To people and moves by which they profoundly believe. Community contractors: responsible, trustworthy, reliable. Hardworking and persevering, sacrificing for the others, they make security and stability within their own world, bringing a combined soul.

Average Degrees

Measure 4: Start Investing their energy and time to anything they believe will probably be stable and safe. Organizing and structuring, they seem to lobbied and governments to get security and persistence. Constantly cautious, expecting issues.

Measure 5: On Resist with more demands made by these, that they react against the others passive-aggressively. Grow evasive, indecisive, attentive, procrastinating, and ambivalent. Are exceptionally reactive, stressed, and unwanted, giving conflicting, "mixed signals" Internal confusion causes them to respond.

Amount 6: On Compensate for jealousy, they get amusing and belligerent, while the others for their own problems, having a hard stance toward "outsiders." Highly reactive and defensive, dividing people into enemies and friends, while on the lookout for dangers with their security. Authoritarian while fearful of jurisdiction, incredibly suspicious, nonetheless, conspiratorial, also fear-instilling to quiet their particular anxieties.

Allergic Levels

Amount 7: Fearing Which they've destroyed their security, they get panicky, volatile, and self-disparaging with extreme inferiority feelings. Watching themselves as defenseless, they search out a stronger ability or opinion to solve all of the issues. Highly divisive, disparaging and others

Grade 8: Feeling Persecuted, others have been "out for them" that they lash-out and behave appropriately, contributing to exactly what they fear. Fanaticism, violence.

Amount 9: Hysterical, and wanting to escape punishment, and they get self-evident and suicidal. Alcoholism, drug overdoses, "skid row," self-abasing behaviour. Generally, contrasts with the passive aggressive and Paranoid personality disorders.

Addictions

Rigidity in diet induces nutrient deficiencies ("that I Do not enjoy veggies"). Working too. Caffeine and amphetamines for endurance, but also alcohol and also depressants to deaden stress. Higher susceptibility to alcoholism compared to many types.

Personal Development Tips

For Enneagram Form Sixes

· Bear in mind there is not anything unusual about being apprehensive since everybody is worried plus a great deal more frequently than you may think. Figure out how to become present to your stress, to research this, and also to come to terms with it. Work creatively with your anxieties without turning into excessive amount of alcohol (or other drugs) to allay them. In reality, if you're breathing and present altogether, stress can be more expressive, a sort of tonic which may make you more productive and more alert to what it is you do.

· You are inclined to find edgy and testy once you're angry or mad and may turn on the others and blame them for all things that you do or caused your own. Be conscious of that your pessimism: it induces you dark moods and unwanted thought patterns you often work on reality. Whenever you succumb to the self-doubt, you may eventually become your worst enemy and can harm yourself more than someone else can.

· Sixes have a tendency to over react if they have been under stress and feeling stressed. Learn how to spot exactly what causes you to over react. Additionally, recognize that nearly none of these situations you have feared a lot of has actually be realized. Even if matters are as awful as you might think, your fearful thoughts disturb you along with your capacity to change matters for the better. You can't always purge outside events, nevertheless, you may manage your thoughts.

· Focus with becoming more expecting. There are several individuals in life it is possible to turn to who worry for you and that are trusted. Otherwise, head out of the best path to find somebody trustworthy, and permit yourself to get near this individual. This will definitely mean risking rejection and waking a number of one's deepest anxieties, however the risk may be well worth taking. You've got a talent for getting people to like you personally, nevertheless, you're not certain of yourself and could be scared of making a commitment in their mind. So, return on one side or another of this fencing on your relationships. Let individuals know exactly how you are feeling about these.

· The others probably think better of you than you realize, and a few folks are really out for you. In reality, your anxieties inform you about your perspectives toward the others than they signify concerning the others' attitudes supporting you personally.

Type 2: The Epicure considers You Have to keep things open and positive to guarantee a Satisfying escape and life out of a world which creates pain and demands limitation. Thus, Epicures are both optimistic, optimistic, joy and potential seeking, and adventuresome, but may be both pain-avoidant, uncommitted, and self-explanatory.

Enneagram Sevens possess the inspirational requirement to encounter Life to the fullest and also steer clear of pain. Sevens appreciate a feeling of focus and freedom on confidence, being motivated and accepting opportunities as they present themselves. Sevens approach life being an experience and love being spontaneous and lively. In their finest, the others are going to experience Sevens as serene and content, once they have the ability to adopt freedom and become gift to the world . At a healthy amount, the others might experience Sevens too spontaneous, uncommitted and unfocused since they're diverted by their search for fulfilment and also a fear of falling out.

The presents of this Enneagram Seven comprise:

· Optimistic: The Seven's focus about which brings happiness, pleasure and happiness to life lets them exude confidence.

· Flexible: Since Sevens are conducive to chances and just like to keep their options available, they are going to soon be flexible facing change, challenges and drawbacks.

· Future-Oriented: By emphasizing what's next, the Seven's visionary and enthusiastic qualities empower them to anticipate and make a fantastic occasion.

· Practical: In their best, Sevens unite their thoughts with an easy and productive attention that allows them to produce things happen.

· Adventurous: as being a lively, versatile and impulsive individual, Sevens frees their liberty and love to explore new lands and adventures.

Average Thinking Patterns:

Sevens possess an energetic head that goes between and joins Thoughts effortlessly. This sort wishes to devote their energy and time into the matters that interest them and reacts immediately to stimulation. The thinking mode, for that reason, combines quick mental processing with a higher demand for emotional stimulation. They desire options and despise feeling which their decisions have been limited or they are now being put somehow. The thinking style permits them to collect a breadth of knowledge across a vast array of subjects. This generalist knowledge may empower innovation and creativity since they've got a large amount of knowledge to join and also draw. Sevens are aroused with their own capacity to build and share a large number of thoughts with other folks. Once they encounter new facts they will process and incorporate it immediately, frequently learning because they move together and from the "doing".

Average Action Patterns:

Sevens get tired easily and dull or repetitive jobs could Have down them. They'll, thus, consciously hunt enthusiasm and Try fresh Things, frequently leaving tasks incomplete since they commence something fresh. Sevens Want to make momentum in life and also behave intelligently to keep matters moving forward. They like the rush of adrenalin that comes with enthusiasm and attempting Something fresh. Under stress Sevens will Multi-task, juggle plans and Could Be Inclined to carry more than is realistic. The entire body of this Seven is likely as busy as your brain. This embodiment of vitality can manifest as active body Language and continuous movement -- many Sevens dislike sitting for longer Than just a few moments. To the others it might seem like Sevens are worried, always juggling actions or in their way someplace.

Average Feeling Patterns:

Sevens resonate together with all the optimistic facet of this psychological Landscape and their saying of these may mostly be lively and optimistic. The others are very likely to see Sevens too joyous, enthusiastic and optimistic. Whether Sevens experience or song in to embarrassing and unwanted emotions like stress depression, despair or anxiety, their instinctive answer is towards favourable chances and plans for future years. This permits them to escape and re-evaluate disquiet. Sevens might also be rather proficient at "reinterpreting" unwanted experiences to frame them as favourable chances or learning adventures. This sort of rationalisation could make it burdensome for a Seven to have full individual responsibility when things fail, but in addition can help maintain them a positive path. Sevens do not enjoy having their skills contested and certainly will eventually become mad if people accomplish this. They will likely consciously function to alter the mood towards something positive and light whenever things get heavy or attempt to lighten the mood by telling jokes.

Blind Spots

· The Seven is quite quick to synthesise and find new facts and techniques. They can, however, overestimate the degree to which they will have truly mastered and consumed this comprehension. They can position themselves as a "instant expert" with no thickness of knowledge that's required for authentic expertise. This can lead individuals to question their own capability and credibility.

· The needs to be busy and participated along with also their exceptionally active human body gestures, communication thoughts and style could be exciting in their mind but may be distracting and bothersome to some others. In case their style contributes to fidgeting or pacing, folks might well not correctly focus on their own thoughts. The Seven may possibly well not know about the degree to which this affects group and other procedures.

· Their busy and speedy mind can lead Sevens to assume they understand exactly what other men and women will express. Consequently, they might well not listen directly to what individuals are actually saying.

· Sevens might desire to feel totally accepting of these, but always avoid things which is going to allow them to feel like that. Back in rationalising mistakes, moving towards favourable emotions and hunting enthusiasm, Sevens may possibly be preventing themselves out of experiencing themselves whole.

· Sevens can hide fear and unwillingness by expressing and pruning into boredom. Once they are feeling fearful of something, they may possibly wind up tuning into the manners this opportunity will confine them in order to avoid confronting their anxieties.

Type 2: Your Protector considers you have to be strong and strong to guarantee a fulfilling lifestyle in a demanding and benign universe in that the powerful will make the most of you personally. Thus, Protectors are justice-seeking, lead, strong, and action-oriented, but could be too impactful, extortionate, and spontaneous.

Eights are self-explanatory strong, strong, and assertive. Protective, resourceful, straight talking, and critical, but may be ego centric and domineering. Eights feel they have to control their environment, notably people, sometimes becoming confrontational and intimidating. Eights typically have difficulties with their tempers as well as letting themselves become more exposed. In their very best: self- respecting, they use their strength to improve others' lives, becoming heroic, magnanimous, and inspirational.

· Fundamental Stress: to Be hurt or controlled from other people

· Fundamental Wish: To shield themselves (to maintain control of their life

And fate)

· Enneagram Eight using a Seven-Wing: "The Maverick"

· Enneagram Eight using a Nine-Wing: "The Bear"

Key Motivations: Wish To be self-indulgent, to establish their potency and also withstand fatigue, to become crucial within their own universe, to control the surroundings, and also to keep in charge of their circumstance.

The Significance of this Arrows (in short)

When going into their Management of Disintegration (anxiety), Selfconfident Eights unexpectedly become pitiful and pitiful in Five. But when moving into their Management of Integration (growth), lustful, controlling Eights become open-hearted and affectionate, such as healthy Twos.

Form Six Overview

Eights have tremendous willpower and energy, and they sense Most residing once they're exercising these abilities on the planet. They utilize their abundant power to influence changes within their own environment --to "leave their mark" about it but and to continue to keep the surroundings, and particularly other men and women, from damaging them and the ones that they care for. In a young period, Eights know this requires endurance, will, dedication, and endurance qualities they develop into themselves and they search for in the others.

Eights Don't Want to be commanded or to let others to Have authority over them (their Fundamental Fear), perhaps the ability is emotional, sexual, social, or even financial. Much of these behaviours is closely associated in ensuring they maintain and increase all power they will have so long as achievable. An afterthought could be an overall or even a gardener, a little entrepreneur or perhaps a mogul, the mum of a family members or the premium of a religious community. No thing: being "accountable" and making their opinion onto their world is uniquely feature of the them.

Eights would be the authentic "rugged individualists" of this Enneagram. More than some other type they stay alone. They would like to be separate and withstand being indebted to anybody. They frequently won't "devote" to societal tradition, plus they're able to withstand shame, anxiety, and also concern regarding the outcome of their activities. Even though they're typically alert to exactly what individuals consider these, they don't enable the opinions of the others influence them. They move about their business using a steely conclusion which could be awe inspiring, actually intimidating to other folks.

Although, to Some Degree, Eights fear bodily injury, much More significant is that their anxiety about getting disempowered or manipulated somehow. Eights are extremely demanding and may consume a good deal of bodily punishment with no criticism --a double-edged blessing simply because they frequently simply take their health insurance and endurance for granted and neglect the wellbeing and also wellbeing of many others also. Yet they're desperately afraid to be hurt emotionally and certainly will use their bodily strength to guard their feelings and keep the others in a safe emotional space. Underneath the challenging façade is exposure, even though it's been covered over by coating of psychological armor.

Ergo, Eights are usually exceptionally industrious, however at the Price of losing contact many of individuals inside their own lives. Those near to these may possibly become increasingly disappointed with this condition of events, that confounds Eights. ("I really don't know what my children is whining about. I bust my hump to supply for them. Why are they frustrated with me personally ")

When This Occurs, Eights feel misunderstood and can Distance themselves farther. Actually, under their counterparts outside, Eights frequently feel rejected and hurt, but that really is something that they seldom speak about because they will have trouble visualizing their exposure to themselves, let alone to anybody. As they fear they will soon be refused (screened, humiliated, and criticized, fired, or hurt somehow), `` Eights make an effort to shield themselves from alerting the others . The outcome is that ordinary Eights eventually become obstructed in their power to get in touch to people or even to love since love delivers the additional power, re-awakening their Fundamental Stress.

The further Eights build their egos so as to shield Themselves, the more sensitive they turn into some imaginary little for their self-respect, ability, or pre-eminence. The longer they try to make themselves more difficult to pain or hurt (whether psychological or physical), the longer they"shutdown" emotionally to eventually become hardened and rock like.

When Eights are mentally fit, nevertheless, they've a Resourceful,"cando" attitude together with a constant internal drive. They accept the initiative and make things happen with a wonderful passion forever. They have been honest and authoritative--ordinary leaders that have a sound, controlling presence. Their groundedness gives them abundant "good sense" and the power to be critical. Eights are eager to "shoot the warmth," comprehending that any decision can't please everybody else. However, just as far as you possibly can, they would like to care for the interests of these people within their bill without even playing favourites. They utilize their skills and fortitude to make a much better world for everyone within their own lives.

Form Six --Quantities of Development

Healthy Degrees

Degree Inch (In Their Most Useful): Become self-restrained and magnanimous, merciful and Forbearing, sparking self by using their self-surrender into a greater jurisdiction. Courageous, prepared to put self into extreme danger to attain their vision and possess an enduring influence. May possibly reach true heroism and dedication that is historical.

Level-2: Self Assertive, Self-confident, and strong:'ve learned to endure for exactly what they desire and need. A resourceful, "can do" attitude and fervent internal drive.

Degree 3: Decisive, Authoritative, and controlling: the organic pioneer the others appear to. Require motivation, create things happen: winner men and women, protective, company, and honest, carrying the others with their own strength.

Average Degrees

Degree 4: Self-sufficiency, Financial freedom, and with enough funds are essential concerns: eventually become pragmatic, pragmatic, and "rugged individualists," wheeler-dealers. Risk-taking, hardworking, denying particular psychological demands.

Measure 5: Begin To control their environment, for example the others: wish to believe others are supporting them, encouraging their own efforts. Swaggering, boastful, strong, and grand: that the "manager" whose word is law. Proud, egotistical, would like to enforce their vision and will to what, perhaps not visiting others as equals or fixing them with respect.

Measure 6: Become Highly combative and debilitating to acquire their manner: confrontational, belligerent, creating new connections. Everything a test of wills, plus they'll not backdown. Use dangers and reprisals to acquire obedience from the others, to keep the others off balance and insecure. But, unjust treatment causes the others fear and resent them possibly additionally group together.

Allergic Levels

Amount 7: Defying Any effort to restrain them become utterly callous, dictatorial,"might makes right" The offender and outlaw, renegade, along with conartist. Hard-hearted, immoral and possibly vicious.

Amount 8: Develop Delusional notions about their ability, invincibility, and capacity to prevail:

megalomania, feeling omnipotent, invulnerable. Recklessly overextending self.

Amount 9: In case They get at threat, they can savagely ruin everything which hasn't conformed with their own will in the place of feign to anybody. Vengeful, barbaric, murderous. Sociopathic tendencies. Generally, corresponds to this Anti-Social Personality Disorder.

Addictions

Blow Off Physiological wants and issues: avert medical visits and check-ups. Founded in abundant foods, alcohol, and tobacco whilst pushing self too much contributes to elevated stress, strokes, and cardiovascular disease. Get a grip on problems essential, even though alcoholism and narcotic dependence are potential.

Personal Growth Tips

The enneagram test

· It goes against the grain but behave with self-restraint. You reveal true power once you forbear from claiming your will with the others, even once you might. Your actual power is based on your power to energize and inspire people. You're in the best when you just take control and help everyone through a catastrophe. Few will make the most of you once you're caring, and also you may do more to safeguard the dedication and dedication of the others by simply revealing the greatness of one's heart than you could by screens of raw strength.

· It's tough to get Eights, but figure out how to return to the others, at the least sporadically. Many times, little is at stake, also you're able to allow the others to get their own manner without even anxiety about forfeiting your power, or even your own real demands. The urge to dominate all of the time can be that an indication your self is starting to match --a threat signal that serious struggles along with the others are inevitable.

· Bear in mind that the globe isn't contrary to you personally. Lots of men and women that you experienced worry for you personally and appear for you personally, however when you're in your own fixation, you don't get this simple for them. Let from the attachment that's available. Doing so won't make you weak but can confirm that the potency and encourage on your own along with your own life. Also bear in mind that by thinking others are against you personally and responding against them you generally alienate them and confirm that your fears. Simply take stock of those men and women who are in your own side and inform them just how important they have been for you.

· Eights typically are interested in being self-reliant and rely upon nobody. But ironically, they be determined by lots of men and women. By way of instance, you can believe that you aren't dependent upon your own employees because they rely upon you to their own jobs. You might dismiss them in any moment and hire different workers. Everybody is expendable on your kingdom--except you. However, the truth is that you're hooked on the others to accomplish their tasks too, especially if your organization concerns grow beyond that which you're able to manage independently. But in the event that you snore everyone connected with you personally, you will gradually be made to apply the many obsequious and un-trustworthy operatives. Whenever you do, then you'll have reason to question your devotion and also to fear losing your own position. The simple fact is that if on your small business or your national existence, your self-sufficiency is primarily an illusion.

· Eights on average over-value power. With power, if wealth, location, or simple brute force, lets them accomplish anything they need, to feel important, to be feared and obeyed. But people that are interested in you due to one's power don't not like you yourself, nor does one like or admire them. While this might be the Faustian bargain you've made, you'll nonetheless need to pay for the purchase price that whatever power you collected will be at a charge for you personally, emotionally and physically.

Type 2: Your Mediator considers You Have to mix in with other people and "go along to get along" To guarantee a fulfilling lifestyle at a universe which causes you to insignificant or requires one to mix. Thus, Mediators are all harmony-seeking, comfortable, and stable, but could be both self-forgetting, conflict-avoidant, and tenacious.

Enneagram Nines are prompted by a requirement to become settled and in harmony with all the entire world and, consequently, being adapting and accepting will probably be crucial in their mind. They try to find a peaceful lifestyle and love equilibrium, preferring to prevent battle. In their finest, Nines are advocated as self-aware and energetic. They supply the present of perfect, sustainable activity to the world. Less-healthy Nines might be advocated as procrastinating, tenacious and self-denying. This stems in the blueprint of moving along to go together with the others along with the eventual distress which appears when this plan isn't satisfying.

The presents of this Enneagram Nine comprise:

· Agreeable: Nines are simple to go on side. Other individuals experience them too open, tranquil and receptive.

· Recognizing: Nines can obey gaps and understand many viewpoints, with a wonderful skill in finding and synthesis commonalities across gaps.

· Patient: Nines do matters in a serene, renewable way, expecting the pure rhythm of processes and projects.

· Supportive: the others believe accepted, understood and heard at the existence of Nines. They accept people for who they truly are and watch their entire potential.

· Actual: Everything you find is exactly what you receive with a Nine plus, so they truly are unpretentious. The others are relaxed using them.

Average Action Patterns:

Enneagram 9 is at the activity center of the Enneagram, however It's the conflicted archetype inside this centre. Nines restrain their environment by simply not allowing the others to get a grip on them typically resisting in a passive method. Their activities, and also usually insufficient activity, will soon be centered on maintaining peace and harmony. Nines shun conflict. They make recognizable rhythms and patterns within their own lives and draw comfort out of the pattern of involvement with their environment and tasks. Nines wish to truly feel close and connected for people, which frequently contributes to a "blending" of energy with all the people nearest to them. This will take the shape of embracing the customs, hobbies, interests and on occasion emotions of those people inside their romantic space.

Average Thinking Patterns:

Nines like structured procedures, details and clarity and Will, consequently, create approaches or customs speedily. In addition, they are inclined to be proficient at coordinating large quantities of detail or information to some coherent arrangement. A Nine may possibly be hard-headed and uncooperative compared to those who do not understand them might repent. They'll rarely express the ideas and self talk they take part in with the others since they usually do not wish to "subject" them into those thoughts lest it boils down them. Nines could be relegated to being marginally disappointed with certain facets of these relationships or life.

Average Feeling Patterns:

Though Nines encounter a Variety of extreme emotions, They endeavour an even-tempered and easy-going demeanour. They'll maintain strong feelings for themselves, allowing the others to go through the Six as really approachable and calm, despite the fact that they could well not feel that this way. Because emotions seem very intense towards the and so they for stability, they encounter most feelings at the lower to medium frequency of strength. Despite their capacity to mediate in conflict situations, Nines dis-like linking with their particular anger. Faith is a very draining experience for Nines, that regularly have some time to observe they are angry. They, thus, do not let themselves undergo anger too frequently or too deeply. Nines "song in" into the emotions and feelings of all those people. Should they have been enthused and energised, then the Six will discuss within this positivity and motivation. Exactly the exact same might happen when people around them feel.

Blind Spots

· Nines you shouldn't be commanded by other people at a counterintuitive method, by being more passive, non-assertive and unmoved. This pattern of in direct behaviour might impact in their relationships and communication.

· Nines desire in order to do not be contentious. Despite disliking it if folks pressurise them to something, they have difficulties saying no to people. While Nines will move out of the way to adapt the others and exude their particular needs, putting up themselves to be overlooked, Nines dislike being discounted.

· Most Enneagram Nines don't know about the particular passive aggressive behaviour patterns and how these affect the others.

· In pursuing their requirement to make sure that everybody is being discovered, Nines frequently present multiple perspectives in conversation with other people. This may possibly cause drawn-out, long explanations which induce the listener to shed interest. In addition, it can impact adversely about the Nine's amount of sway and also credibility.

· Being accommodating, Nines can don't make their real needs, feelings and desires called the people round them. The Nine might believe they are doing very obviously, but because of their approach, the others might overlook what they truly desire and desire. It might also be the all these feelings and needs are being articulated from the Nine's mind and perhaps not being distributed to the others as publicly and as usually as they presume.

Along with focusing on the two Kinds of core opinion Patterns, the Enneagram system works together with 3 centres of Intellect --mind, heart, and body--and also the 3 basic aversive emotions Related to all these centres of intellect --panic, distress, and anger. All of us Have a number of every enter us, however it is vital that you figure out that a customer's center Type as, as the following case illustrates it gives us leverage Which to encourage the task of individual transformation.

CHAPTER THREE

HOW CAN YOU FIGURE OUT WHAT TYPE OF PERSONALITY YOU ARE?

The Enneagram can be a potent personality typing tool utilized by trainers and others interested in spiritual and personal growth. From the Enneagram, you can find eight different character types and about three centres - or - triads - of - intellect, for example heart disease and gut. And at each triad you can find 3 various personality types.

From the Heart Tri Ad lie types 3, 2, and 4. Type two may be that the Giver, 3 is currently your Performer, and 4 might be the Romantic (also sometimes called "Tragic Romantic"). We all feel at home inside their emotion centre or one's center.

All these Three types possess a psychological thermometer that's moving to the entire world and analysing everybody else it lumps in to. They enter to a space and it's really almost like that they could probe individuals who live in the space. They are going right through questions such as, "Are they feeling? Just how are they responding for me personally? What's their mentally content?"

Type S 3, 2, and 4 - it is about Graphic

Type S two, 3, and 4 would be one's core triad and therefore are emotion-based. They believe at home, getting together with all the world through emotion, and so they have been dedicated to image - to how they're perceived.

They're Perhaps not only in song with your answers or emotional content, but they are also always correcting themselves as they truly are worried about the way you're reacting to them. They truly are continuously adapting themselves into exactly what perceive are the psychological responses. Every one of those 3 types look different once they perform it.

Type S two, 34 and 4 possess an inherent belief they will need to make significance or perhaps a feeling of worth. Their internal awareness of self is basically determined on which exactly is reflected straight back to them. Exactly what the outside world sees inside these becomes that they're. This is really where their attention is drawn - to other's emotional reaction for them. They're centered about the things they do and state - the way they job and hold themselves. It's all about looks.

And also this "image thing" continues on and off. It's reflected from the vitality that they put out, the way in which they walk and so they way they proceed. It's even from the jargon that they utilize; as an instance, you're able to find Sort 3 (Achiever) picking up the jargon in a particular category or social circumstance.

Type 4 is in contact whatever somebody could say that could make them feel less - or on the surface - the bunch. Emotionally-they will have this massive reactivity for the and answer for this.

And Type 2's are focusing to all of the emotions everyone has been having, and what's happening to them. They are asking, "How do I help out you and you are your requirements " It's all tuned into emotion; this is exactly why it's known as the Picture Point - they have been creating their image dependent on the emotional way the others answer them.

Under The face of two's, 3's and 4 is that there was shame and despair. While they start doing their job, they'll normally bulge into inherent indications of pity of that they are, in order to see they have paid by looking for some other person.

Their Notions are running across the lines of, "There's something down there that's just not right inside me. I cannot let people in too close because internal flaw may possibly be discovered. They are able to come from, but only maybe not too close. They may detect that thing"

Types 5, 6 and 7 - the Emotional Tri Ad

Type S 5, 7 and 6 would be the head-based types, having an abysmal of anxiety and fear.

They reside from the area of believing, cognition and strategizing. The move they will have made into the mind is all about creating control and safety at the place where they won't be "down from the cluttered emotions" where they've been unmanageable along with getting together with "other activities" outside from the whole world.

Their Notions go something like, "Up from the mind I will attempt to know it. I am able to think through matters. I am able to cause a model for the way this universe works and I impose my version on the Earth, and that I start to trust the version much more I think that the world"

The Emotional kinds have been strategizes - frequently skilful players. They know the entire world and societal situations throughout the mind instead of throughout one's center (emotions) are human anatomy (intestine). They have been attending to through eyes. They have been watching and celebrating to answer questions such as "Just how are people responding - at a believing way - if you ask me personally " And "What is happening?"

For many the head kinds, there's generally a standard mistrust of earth. For the 5, folks come too close and there's an association. Out of this, mistrust grows plus also they escape from the world included in their own strategy.

Type 6 Are moving in and out, however their mistrust has gone outside there on earth. They are thinking, "I cannot expect." Nonetheless, it is also an inside awareness, therefore they are even thinking, "I cannot believe." Ergo there's a great deal of dichotomy in the half of the

The 7 is More of the externalized trust. Their focus of attention has gone outside from the entire world, sometimes giving away their authority but not feeling more comfortable using this. Afterward your anxieties and also the anxieties can attest out from the planet, more they are able to indoors.

Type-S 8, 9 and 1 - at the Human Body and Gut

Type S 8, 9 and 9 would be your human anatomy (or intestine)-established kinds) They believe matters throughout the human anatomy. They make lively hits. Once they head into an area, it isn't all about the emotion or believing; rather, they are wondering, "How can this person feel in my experience down here within my own intestine?"

For your Body kinds, there's an inherent anger or bitterness which frequently turns up as ruling. For Sort 9, if anger becomes repressed, they don't really actually allow out it. Along with also their demands become repressed.

Should you Speak to a "young 9" starting to complete their private work, they'll likely answer, "Anger, exactly what are you discussing? I am definitely the most tender, happy-go-lucky, calm man I understand. I don't understand anger.

However, as They go deeper to themselves which anger becomes more apparent and can be frequently a gate way for them. They'll undergo a completely different degree of self-awareness along with saying. For first time in their own lives, they'll know what their demands are and everything they need.

Type 8 Often externalize the anger. Their energy is a lot bigger also it arrives. It might overwhelm anger and people may flooding into the globe. In addition, they often have a feeling of other's borders. They obtain their anger outside and enjoy confronting the others precisely the exact same way.

Type 1 Turn the anger inward. They'll clarify an interior politician - a voice that is stressing - which will be riding them. It's often saying something such as, "You need to get it done such a way. That really is everything you went wrong. You're dumb. You do not achieve so correctly. You're not affective enough. You aren't energized. You're perhaps not (anything) enough.

This Anger is internalized, however frequently they may likewise be rather judgmental and critical of different folks. There's really a rebellious inner component in their opinion. Type 1 often hold on the anger inside their body.

Therefore people Are the three"Centers of Intelligence" - one's core (Forms 2, 3 and 4 having an inherent despair or pity), the mind (types 5, 6, and 7 having an inherent fear or stress), and also your human anatomy (types 8, 9 and inch having inherent anger or conclusion).

Self-knowledge Can be enabling, and also the Enneagram is intended to help you in discovering some crucial sections of yourself which might well not be instantly obvious. It can inform you in your inclinations -- exactly what you're very likely to decide on if presented using various choices. In addition, it lets you know regarding your deeper life targets, your own wants and notably the worth. Your worth what you strive for and will be able to allow you to describe your targets.

It will Perhaps not but inform you of the type of skills you've got, and just how you've learned. Neither does this have to say regarding your abilities; for instance, if you are good with numbers or possess exemplary spatial abilities.

The Enneagram can provide the following advantages on your own life and operate:

Fosters Self-awareness and Valuable introspection

Let's you know just how a World may look from different viewpoints

It allows one to make fresh, Positive behaviours

It allows one to discover and break loose from routines

It can help you're longer Compassionate and understanding among the others

CHAPTER FOUR

Help with identifying your enneagram

Ones are a body-based kind having an emphasis on private Ethics and self-control. Their attention extends toward visiting and correcting what's wrong, and also doing the ideal thing. They're famous for their honesty, dependability and ordinary sense.

Ones Are Extremely accountable, so much so That They Might resent Additional men and women who do not enjoy life as badly as they perform. They have standards and have a tendency to find things in black and white, wrong and right. It's simple to allow them to become more very important, of others and themselves. They work hard at being right constantly. They have been idealistic and certainly will exert great effort to boost the world over them, which frequently places them at the function of social bookmarking. Their key components of growth would be to understand how to just accept their imperfections and endure other people's points of perspective.

Strengths: Honest, responsible, improvement-oriented

Issues: Resentful, Non-adaptable, and too critical

Discussing design: Precise and detail-oriented, using a tendency to sermonize

Lower psychological dependency: Resentment, that results in becoming mad but carrying it in

Higher E Motion: Serenity, that includes letting go of anger in regards to how things are and accepting imperfection

Archetypal question: To alter everything could be altered, to take everything can't be Changed, and also to build up the intellect to learn the gap

Emotional defenses: Ones utilize the defense mechanisms of response formation to prevent Their anger (along with other instincts and feelings) and also take care of the personal image of being "right." (Reaction formation is still sensing a single thing and doing precisely the alternative, like feeling resentful but behaving fine).

Somatic patterns: As Body-based types, Ones usually are educated and practical, proficient in arranging the activities of everyday life. The pressure to become right and also the significance of hands contributes to physical rigidity and strain, especially in the neck, neck, back and shoulders. The face area could simply take in a manifestation of mad conclusion or resentful martyrdom.

Defense Mechanism

Reaction formation -- atmosphere something and expressing the exact reverse

Ones Utilize response formation to Prevent direct anger and also to Get a grip on their instincts and emotions. This can help them maintain a self-image of remaining right. The constant need of this inner critic must be "good" frequently replaces personal requirements and shuts down feelings.

2. HELPER

Twos are a feeling-based type using a focus on relationship. They do well in making relations and socialize together with the demands and feelings of other men and women. They're typically very good at encouraging helping and others draw out their possibility. But, turning their attention toward themselves and knowing exactly what they need is quite a bit harder. They would like to become accepted and enjoyed by the others, plus so they are going to accommodate or change to get paid this particular approval.

A Little like psychological sponges, Twos Must Be very careful What they consume from the folks around them. Getting mad or putting personal bounds can be exceedingly tough to complete, though they could have emotional outbursts to alleviate the pressure. While being truly a unique person or getting the approval of the others has its own advantages, it will not replacement being adored on your own.

Strengths: Caring, Popular, singer

Issues: Privileged, Naive, determined

Discussing design: Be-ing Fine and sympathetic, giving information, sometimes militant for your own reason

Lower psychological dependency: Pride about becoming particular, significant, or crucial in Dating. Or Inadequate self-respect if acceptance Isn't coming

Higher E Motion: Humility, which will be having the ability to understand and grip on the adventure of self-worth without self-inflation or extortionate self-judgment

Archetypal question: To locate oneself in connection, balancing dependence and Freedom

Emotional defenses: Twos utilize the defense mechanisms of repression to prevent their Own wants and feelings also to keep the self-image to be "helpful." (Repression is putting the improper feelings from understanding and turning them into a more acceptable form of psychological vitality).

Somatic patterns: As Feeling forms, Twos undergo a buildup of energy, and at times strain, round their torso and diaphragm. Even though high in energy inside their upper bodies, it's hard to allow them to feel their bodies and keep grounded. They are inclined to release their stress thru talking and emoting. It's simple to allow them to"somatize" or convert hidden/repressed feelings to physical signs or symptoms.

3. PERFORMER

Threes are all feeling-based forms, however they channel their Emotional energy to getting stuff done. They simply take the initiative and work hard to reach their own targets. They have been exceptionally elastic, and so they do well in "feeling out" and fulfilling the expectations of the others when which may make them victory. They prefer to keep busy and, on the move, therefore it's tough to slow or stop down. Their concentrate on keeping their image up and achieving consequences can enter the form of personal requirements and health.

American Company Is an especially powerful three culture Where actors receive yourself a great deal of positive reinforcement to being productive and productive. A threat for Threes is centering on outside compliments or substance rewards while losing touch who they've been indoors. It's problematic to allow them to measure out of these functions, feel their own feelings, and decide for themselves exactly what is vital.

Strengths: Powerful, Lively, higher achiever

Issues: Over Functioned, Ranked, aggressive

Discussing design: Enthusiastic, inspiring others and themselves for achievement

Lower psychological dependency: Vanity, predicated on maintaining up a Fantastic picture and constantly being Powerful

Higher E Motion: Truthfulness, that could be your willingness to move beyond looks and develop exclusive validity

Archetypal question: To Give up picture and societal character and locate one's internal Character

Emotional defenses: Threes utilize the defense mechanisms of identification to prevent Failure and keep up a self-image to be "successful" (Identification can be a sort of pervading roleplaying and losing in image).

Somatic patterns: As Feeling kinds that put everything to results and productivity, Threes can accrue lots of strain around their torso and center. They really are the initial "Form a's" and will need to be on the lookout for premature heart attacks or perhaps a diminished immune process. Under a powerful coating of torso strain there's usually profound despair in loss of touch with an inner self.

4. ROMANTIC

Fours are all feeling-based kinds who frequently experience a feeling of yearning and depression. Something is missing for these, and this can result in a pursuit of wholeness through romantic idealism, healing, or even aesthetics. If they compare themselves with the others, Fours experience feelings of jealousy. They hunt depth and meaning within their customs, their job, or within a pursuit for individual imagination.

Most Fours are musicians that excel in expressing global Human emotions in dancing, songs, and even poetry. While they search to get a great image, it's most essential that they be more true. Frequently enthused, sometimes too emotional, their attention goes forward and backward from empathizing with the others with their inner experience. They require time. The trick to growth and healing to Fours will be always to restrain melancholy together with the capability of enjoyment and gratification, even in the event the romantic relationship or your knowledge appears faulty or faulty.

Strengths: Compassionate, Idealistic, emotional thickness

Issues: Moody, Retreated, un-cooperative

Discussing design: Sometimes warm and feelingful, occasionally dry and flat; they often Be abstract, plus so they strive to be correct. Many times, a tone of despair or dissatisfaction

Lower psychological dependency: Envy or depression as a Result of the encounter of Disappointment or lack

Higher E Motion: Equanimity, so keeping one's center open, relaxed all emotions nevertheless residing in balance

Archetypal challenge: Managing an open center when incorporating pleasure and anguish

Emotional defenses: Fours utilize the defense mechanisms of introjection to prevent being Ordinary also to keep a self-image to be "authentic." (Introjection is your endeavor to conquer absence by earning value from out oneself in addition to that the tendency of internalizing blame for what goes wrong).

Somatic designs: Fours Often swing out of touch into withdrawal, from having plenty of feelings which trickle out to the environment for becoming resigned and gloomy. Their energy frequently collects at the center of the human body and will be removed from the periphery (eyes, hands (and feet). Self-expression throughout music, dancing, composing, creative parenting or work helps create a psychological flow and also a balanced condition.

5. OBSERVER

Five S are psychological types who concentrate on intellectual Understanding and collecting knowledge. They have been frequently technical or scholars experts due to their keen understanding and analytical skill. Privacy and private liberty are extremely crucial to these, and also other men and women could possibly be experienced as intrusive. The capacity to detach from different people and out of emotional pressure confers own freedom but might also make loneliness.

Some individuals of the Type Might Be intellectually brilliant or Knowledgeable, while relationships and feelings pose a massive challenge. For many others, friends and family are extremely important, however they are going to still need plenty of time to pursue their particular interests and re-create themselves. Five S will need to balance their inclination to withdraw or subtract from those by contacting the others, even though that calls for disquiet or battle.

Strengths: Scholarly, Perceptive, self-reliant

Issues: Isolated, Too intellectual, stingy

Discussing style: Reasonable and technical, many comfortable inside their region of expertise. Perhaps not big on "little talk"

Lower psychological dependency: Avarice or hoarding, so holding back and forth holding to info, timing, as well as other tools depending on the fear of lack, either on your own or the surroundings.

Higher E Motion: Non-attachment, that will be letting go to be designed for replenishment.; expecting that there's enough.

Archetypal question: Taking Part in existence with feelings, also incorporating the internal and outer worlds

Emotional defenses: Five S utilize the defense mechanisms of isolation to prevent emotions of emptiness also to keep a self-image to be "knowledgeable" and self-adequate. (Isolation could be physical separation, however in addition, it means being cut away in the emotions).

Somatic designs: Five S Often get stuck inside their minds. It will take effort to attract attention into your own human body as well as the emotions. Energy is removed from the periphery of their human body and accumulates from the center. Very sensitive to noise, touch, people, etc., they hold the majority of these tension from the intestine as opposed to from the musculature, even though the ribcage might be quite stiff based on the degree of fear within your system. Five S often "disappear completely" supporting their eyes.

6. LOYAL SKEPTIC

Sixes are psychological types Using their understanding and Intelligence to know the entire world and determine if other men and women are favorable or aggressive. They concentrate on safeguarding the protection of the team, community or project. Sixes are proficient at anticipating issues and inventing solutions. Knowing the guidelines and making arrangements along with different people is crucial, yet in precisely the exact same time they have a tendency to overlook themselves and wonder the others. They are able to differentiate between certainty and doubt, rebel or accurate apology.

Many Sixes Come at the "careful" manner; they Hesitate they worry a whole lot, plus so they still procrastinate. Additional Sixes like to remain in the "potency" manner: they rush to actions and so they attempt to brace themselves ideologically being a means of overcoming their fear. Since Sixes learn how to trust themselves in addition to some other folks, they eventually become flexible and so they also develop the guts to behave even in the existence of uncertainty or ambivalence.

Strengths: Loyal, Courageous, careful to people and issues; frequently strategic leaders

Issues: Suspicious, Alright, suspicious

Discussing design: Putting limitations on others and themselves, having severe questions, and playing devil's advocate. Sometimes ideologically zealous.

Lower psychological dependency: Suspicion or doubt, that may lead to fearfulness and holding an aggressive and pushy attitude

Higher E Motion: Courage, which isn't bravado but alternatively means sense that the panic and moving forwards any way

Archetypal question: To preserve faith in others and also the Lifeforce, and also to Overcome the mind/body split up

Emotional guards: Sixes utilize the protection mechanisms of projection to prevent Personal rejection and keep up a self-image to be "loyal" (Projection can be actually a method of attributing others which you cannot accept on your own, both negative and positive qualities).

Somatic patterns: The Attentive or phobic Sixes have panic covering their own faith and their body-based instincts. They are inclined to stress and worry. In comparison, the counter-phobic Sixes have aggression in addition to these own fears. They have an inclination to rush ahead and bracing themselves mentally to plan your risks. (Most Sixes return forth and back from attentive to counter-phobic). Concerning body armor, the eyes could become questionable and safeguarded, or protruding and fearful. Myopia is not uncommon. The diaphragm may take a whole lot of tension, leading to a staccato or stopping kind of movement and speech.

7. EPICURE

Sevens are psychological types That Are forward thinkers and Forward movers. They generally attract a positive and positive attitude to all or any their tasks. They truly are interested in lots of diverse areas. They don't really want to become restricted by doing just one thing and so they want to maintain their options and chances available.

Although they may be outstanding communicators, they're somewhat less Concerned with picture along with different people's consent compared to other styles. It's crucial that you have pleasure (or have to perform one's own thing), if that is seen in traveling and experience or even maybe more intellectual pursuits. They have been passionate consumers of fresh thoughts, new technology, and experiences that are gratifying. But a lot of a great thing might be an issue for them. Due to their attention changes so fast, it's hard to allow them to get in to matters in detail and also to stay the path in relationships and work. Slowing, being at the present time, and understanding how to endure their very own and also other people's anguish -- all could bring essential equilibrium.

Strengths: Adventurous, Fun-loving, fast believing

Issues: Self-absorbed, Dispersed, uncommitted

Discussing design: Personal Story Telling, that is very amusing or Simply self-absorbed. They also concentrate on the positive, and also have a tendency to discount or fast "reframe" the unwanted.

Lower psychological dependency: Gluttony, which Isn't just about food but rather a Sort of Intoxication or more ingestion of thoughts, interesting experiences or compounds

Higher E Motion: Sobriety, so both limiting ingestion and quieting your mind so as to be found in as soon as

Archetypal question: to Generate idealism sensible, incorporating optimism and optimistic Thinking with the shadow negative or issues

Emotional guards: Sevens utilize the protection mechanisms of rationalization to prevent Anguish and also to keep a self-image to be "okay." (Rationalization can be a way of describing or justifying so as to eliminate pain or denying to accept responsibility.)

Somatic patterns: For Sevens, electricity and attention have a tendency to really go "out and up" in the place of "in and down." Compared to this Five S, energy goes into the periphery of their body away from the center. Sevens have a tendency to keep over-stimulated together with thoughts, compounds, or experiences based on their physique. They're referred to as big talkers. They're frequently quite loose and elastic. As an alternative of muscle strain, their struggle would be "being at" their own bodies and becoming helpless.

8. PROTECTOR

Eights are a body-based kind who are inclined to take control of Situations and measure into a leadership job. They have been intense and lively, and they could be intimidating occasionally to additional men and women. Impatient with regulations and rules, they prefer to do things in their way. By claiming control over their environment, they really do their very best to protect themselves and other people that is a portion of these loved ones or group.

Fairness or citizenship is a priority. Should they are feeling Wronged, they are going to struggle since their experience vulnerability or weakness could precipitate an attack against the surface world. The potency (and aggression) which can be generated inside this assignment can be commendable, but additionally misapplied. The task to Eights will be always to unite assertion and restrain with interdependency and collaboration, in addition to learning how to suppress their frequently excessive appetites.

type and identifying your personality

Strengths: Enthusiastic, Generous, strong

Issues: Extortionate, Mad, dominating

Discussing style: Eights usually speak assertively and implement strong direction. They Often be more bossy so when things fail, they frequently become mad.

Lower psychological dependence: Anger and excessiveness, using a revengeful attitude toward people

Higher E Motion: Innocence, so to handle life with an open center and without cynicism

Archetypal question: To exploit Living force in effective ways, including Self-assertion with vulnerability

Emotional defenses: Eights utilize the defense mechanisms of jealousy to prevent Vulnerability and keep up a self-image to be "strong" (Denial can be actually a type of strong re directing of attention and atmosphere predicated on willfulness and restrain).

Somatic designs: Eights Often maintain a high amount of bio-energetic control inside their own bodies. They're brought to strength, plus so they become tired or impatient very readily. This is caused over exertion and/or over consumption. Quick to anger, they could have trouble with impulse control. Their armor turns up as density or strain less or more evenly distributed throughout the human body. It's simple to be rough, hard to become more exposed but softer feelings and demands tend to be present profound within the interior. Eights are famous for its fierceness they (can) express by using their eyes.

9. MEDIATOR

Balanced at the Peak of the Enneagram, Nines would be the very best Basic and many various personality kinds. They really are the "salt of this earth" and the "glue" that holds the city together. People with this kind is available in all sizes and shapes, however they share a frequent problem with inertia (or momentum). Whether they have been idle in the conventional feel or hard workers always on the go, "Nines" are having issues finding and sticking in their particular priorities. It's tough to change guidelines or shift awareness of that which is important. They "forget" themselves.

Nines do well in seeing points of perspective. This will make it Difficult to allow them to create personal conclusions, but at exactly the exact same time frame, they are sometimes exemplary mediators and peacemakers others. Nines seek stability within their environment and can go to great lengths in order to prevent battle (even at occasions (the others). They truly are body-based types, with a powerful gut feel of knowing, even though they are also out of touch with their health.

Strengths: Balanced, accepting, harmonious

Issues: Stubborn, Ambivalent, battle avoidant

Discussing design: Inclusive and relaxing in their finest, Nines could have difficulty Getting into the purpose. They are able to be optional and over-controlled, or else they are sometimes very dispersed.

Lower psychological dependency: Laziness of focus, followed closely by stubbornness, which makes it Hard to allow them to handle priorities or mandatory battle

Higher E Motion: Right Activity, that's the openness to complete what has to be achieved and utilize yourself nicely from the procedure

Archetypal question: Getting out of Bed to priorities at the current instant, incorporating Stability with battle

Emotional guards: Nines utilize the protection mechanisms of narcotization to prevent Battle (from within or without) and also to keep up a self-image to be "comfortable/harmonious." (Narcotization is using food and beverage, studying, television, or even simply just repetitive patterns of doing and thinking to put oneself at a country of decreased consciousness and sense).

Somatic designs: Nines Tend to remain comfortably under-charged. Great at tummy breathing, they could prevent Breathing to the torso area. Low electricity Nines suffer with inertia and bodily Laziness, while high-energy Nines have a tendency to continually release as a way to maintain A secure balance. The back is also an especially vulnerable region. Since Nines Therefore readily combine or "combine" together with others or the surroundings from their stomach center, they will have trouble setting good personal Boundaries.

CHAPTER FIVE

Type On Your Own The Results And After Getting The Results

Have You spent hours onto a jigsaw puzzle simply to understand that an important bit is overlooking? Your first answer might be: "It cannot be overlooking. It has to be here somewhere" You select up every available part in turn. You hunt under the dining table and round the ground. You run your hands across the completed portions of the mystery, trusting your palms will notice something that your eyes have overlooked.

You can walk off from a Jig Saw Mystery that's missing a bit. It's more difficult to leave from the expectation your own life should get together in a purposeful whole. The Enneagram is a system for considering individual nature and motivation which helps people understand the routines within their lives as well as the lives of men and women all over them. Lots of men and women utilize the Enneagram to detect that the bit they were fearful that they were overlooking.

Dependent on a mix of Ancient wisdom and modern scientific science, the Enneagram can be just a version that clarifies the routines people on average use to motivate themselves and relate with the others and face dangers or barriers. The middle of the technique could be that the realization that the plans that work great for people finally also come to be the fault lines which render us exposed. We don't necessarily have advantages and flaws: sometimes the exact grade is both a strength and a weakness.

It's 1 thing to overcome your flaws. It's still another thing entirely to overcome your strengths. The Enneagram will describe you in relation to what you would like, everything you fear, and what exactly it is that you're going to complete to attain results you prefer. It's lively in how people are lively; the Enneagram explains the way we shift if we feel stressed or secure, and also, we proceed between different selves in distinct contexts. A ring with two points, the Enneagram clarifies us all included in a single whole, a person family in that many of us are related and connected.

Much Information Regarding this Enneagram can be obtained on the web and throughout bookstores. There are lots of tests you could take which may start you in the trail to understanding your Enneagram style. Within the subject of Enneagram studies, evaluations are just hints: they signify a starting place and not really a decision. There's not any replacement for speaking about your routines along with different students from the Enneagram. As you have identified yourself throughout your loved ones and work relationships, then you're able to best distinguish yourself over the Enneagram convention by obtaining the view of different people on the routines you really have been living.

A Good weekend Program With a fantastic facilitator will permit one to see yourself and also to find out more in different men and women. You'll start to determine new parts of one's very own personal mystery and also to observe exactly the manner which other men and women are building very different mysteries inside their own lives. You are going to have brand new outlook to encourage new quality on your comprehension of your own and your relationship to other folks.

Should you sometimes feel like You're Missing a crucial part of one's private puzzle, think about learning more in regard to the Enneagram. You may create a fresh awareness of how the routines in Your own life span and join to make a coordinated whole. You may create a Brand-new comprehension of the routines in different people's behaviors. Now you Will plant the seeds to get revived pride and enthusiasm since you build and sustain relationships.

CONCLUSION

Therefore, You're an absolute Newcomer at The Enneagram... You have discovered how beautiful and helpful it may be, however you are not really certain exactly what the big deal is... Well, should you'd like to receive the basics of the Enneagram, then pull a seat up and continue reading.

Before I move on, I want to Say That we now have a range of unique approaches to translate that which we do understand about the enneagram. There are some different "schools of thought" on the subject that you can no doubt find more concerning since you delve deeper into the topic. With that said, what you're about to learn is jaded, opinionated, just partly educated, but just enough to provide you a taste of the Enneagram. And more important- provides one of the push digs deeper.

The Enneagram, actually, is a symbol. It's a nine-pointed emblem that's shown up in lots of religions throughout the past couple of millennia. Nobody knows for certain the ancients developed the analysis or the way they used it before very recently. Enneagram Spectrum sums up the speculations concerning the roots of this enneagram such as this:

"The origins of this Enneagram are disputed. Some writers believe they've discovered variations of this Enneagram emblem while in the sacred geometry of the Pythagoreans that 4000 decades past were interested at the deeper meaning and need for amounts. The lineup of mysterious mathematics was passed through Plato, his disciple Plotinus, and also following Neo-Platonists.

Some think this convention found Its way to esoteric Judaism through Philo, a Jewish Neo-Platonist philosopher," at which it later looks since the Tree of Life from the Cabalistic tradition of ninefoldness.

Variations of the emblem too Seem in Muslim Sufi customs, possibly coming there throughout the philosopher al-Ghazzali. Throughout the fourteenth century that the Naqshbandi Order of Sufism, variously called the "Brotherhood of the Bees" (because they accumulated and stored comprehension) and the "Symbolists" (because they educated through symbols) would be claimed to have passed and preserved the Enneagram logo.

Speculation has it that the Enneagram Found its way to esoteric Christianity during Pseudo-Dionysius (who had been influenced by the Neo-Platonists) and throughout the mysterious Ramon Lull (who had been influenced by his own Muslim studies)

To the frontispiece of some Text Book Written from the nineteenth century by the Jesuit mathematician and also student of arithmology Athanasius Kircher, an Enneagram-like figure looks."

Lately, the Enneagram has been "re discovered" from Oscar Ichazo, a Chilean philosopher who taught in the Arica Institute at Chile. Ichazo, in my opinion, was that the first man to really use the legislation of this enneagram into the nine legislation which operate within the individual mind.

The method by which in which the enneagram is comprehended today is it is an instrument to help comprehend and pronounce nine "filters" that somebody can utilize to find the globe. These filters are somewhat fluid, intangibles which might or might not exist in reality, but with these as tools may cause extreme realizations in relationships or even on your own personal growth.

I believe likening these filters to "os's" of servers is an excellent solution to comprehend it. More than a few folks are running Windows, a few folks are running Linux, plus a few individuals are having an Apple computer keyboard. It has all merely various techniques to carrying the sensory input signal, organizing it, and responding.

The attractiveness of this analysis is that When you're able to pronounce the deepest feelings and secrets of friends and family, family members, and also yourself, you attain a view which was not there before. You end up plainly. Just like before...

Various schools accept the Enneagram In lots of diverse guidelines. Some offer ideas for the best way best to attain expert victory, some give it to life-coaches to help their customers with the info. Some push you for some constraints by choosing the areas on your personality that could use forming up. And several schools do a number of different activities which are beyond the domain with the Complete Beginner's Guide. They are there for one to find, love, and record back about.

I would like to Say for you personally That this really is simply the briefest of overviews. There's just a good deal more to know and live before you begin to reap the advantages of this Enneagram. However, I will promise you, together with the full energy and time along with self-awareness, the Enneagram can be actually a course toward peace and bliss more powerful than whatever I've ever discovered.